T0162991

Healing
Divination

Healing
Divination

Shirley Laboucane

Winchester, UK
Washington, USA

First published by Dodona Books, 2013
Dodona Books is an imprint of John Hunt Publishing Ltd., Laurel House, Station Approach,
Alresford, Hants, SO24 9JH, UK
office1@jhpbooks.net
www.johnhuntpublishing.com
www.dodona-books.com

For distributor details and how to order please visit the 'Ordering' section on our website.

Text copyright: Shirley Laboucane 2012

ISBN: 978 1 78099 459 8

All rights reserved. Except for brief quotations in critical articles or reviews, no part of this
book may be reproduced in any manner without prior written permission from the publishers.

The rights of Shirley Laboucane as author have been asserted in accordance with the Copyright,
Designs and Patents Act 1988.

A CIP catalogue record for this book is available from the British Library.

Design: Stuart Davies

Printed in the USA by Edwards Brothers Malloy

We operate a distinctive and ethical publishing philosophy in all
areas of our business, from our global network of authors to
production and worldwide distribution.

CONTENTS

Introduction   1

Chapter 1 — Decisions   **3**

Chapter 2 — Purification, Prayer & Protection   **9**
Something to Consider for Yourself and a Client   16

Chapter 3 — Angels, Guides & Totems   **18**

Chapter 4 — Angel Medicine   **25**
Healing Meditation: Exercise with Angels   28
Anam Cara: Soul Friend   30
Meditation for Recognizing Various Vibrations of Energy   31

Chapter 5 — Deer Medicine   **32**

Chapter 6 — Swan Medicine   **40**

Chapter 7 — The Green Intuitive   **51**

Chapter 8 — The Aura   **57**
Layers of the Aura and the Chakras   63
The Chakra System   64
Aura Color Meanings   65

Chapter 9 — Playing Card Meanings (Cartomancy)   **68**
Cartomancy: Learning the Meanings of the Cards   72
Mini Celtic Cross   82

**Chapter 10 — Creating and Working with Your
   Own Oracle Deck**   **85**
Dragonfly Medicine Cards   85
Dragonfly Oracle Deck Meanings   87
Meaning of the Seven Directions Cards   89
Earth Teachers Oracle Deck   90
Karma Cards   110
The Seven Directions Reading   116

Chapter 11 — Healing Ritual   **121**

Chapter 12 — Doing a Reading   **124**

Dedication

In gratitude to my mother and mentor Lena Laboucane, whose love and strength still sustains me.

Introduction

The purpose of writing this book was to share the knowledge that I have gained while being a professional reader for over ten years. This book will teach you practical techniques to help you become intuitive. I will guide you through the exercises in developing the three big C's — clairvoyance, clairsentience and clairaudience. I will also teach you how divination can be used as a tool for healing.

As an aboriginal person, I was taught at a young age that it is natural to interact with the beings of this world such as the plants and animals. I believe there is a beautiful connection that exists between all living things, so whether I am seeking guidance from the spirit of the Deer or tuning into the Angelic Realm there is healing to be given and medicine to be received.

Life is a journey. We can create a better existence for ourselves when we look at ourselves honestly. Divination can help us to focus our energies to make positive changes in our lives. The cards are powerful guides/tools to show us how to live in alignment with our own essence.

What if you could unlock your inner psychic self and become more intuitive for the benefit of yourself and others? I have developed my own style of reading that I believe can help you unlock your psychic potential.

Many people are reading this and wondering if this going to take years to accomplish, the answer to that is ... no it does not. The technique I use is just learning how to relax your mind, to focus, to listen and to feel. It's all in the heart; it's all about feeling and sensing energy.

Developing second sight is an ancient knowledge that many cultures have used throughout history. Seers were often chosen because of their bloodline, but today we are becoming more and more aware of just how connected we truly are and how we are all born knowing.

Learning to be more intuitive means more than just learning to tap into someone's energy or to feel the memories that a certain object holds. While those things are fascinating and a huge part of developing your psychic abilities, there is a much deeper element to it, a more profound side to it

Opening yourself up to live more intuitively is not just a journey of self-discovery, but also the realization that we all are born with an innate knowledge of ourselves and others. We are all connected.

Chapter 1

Decisions

Choose what you love...

The first time I had a psychic reading I was around 13 years old. My mother had fallen out with my father and like always, her eccentric friend Trudy was there to be a shoulder to cry on and provide a place to stay. Whenever my mother and her friends came together, there was the usual trip to a psychic followed by coffee shop chatter on men, the newest affairs, and who was breaking up with whom. I loved those times and on my 13th birthday, I was to be welcomed into the fold and was allowed to have my tealeaves read.

I will never forget going for my first reading with the psychic. She lived in the country and yes, I know it sounds like a cliché, but she lived near a swamp and it was spooky. We arrived on time, which was an extraordinary feat for Trudy, the car turned off the road and onto a driveway bordered with wild flowers. Trudy parked the car, and while my mother and her friend smoked cigarettes, I stared out the back window. I felt excited and jittery as I was being initiated into the fold of womanhood. I was grown up. Like a rite of passage, I was now one of the girls and I could participate in those delicious conversations, and it was all so tantalizing and fun.

The spring night was mild and the fog slowly crept in from the swamp and into the atmosphere causing us to feel secluded from the outside world. Its icy strands surrounded the old car and even my mother remarked it was creepy. We got out and headed for the house, in the distance we heard the hoot from an owl and of course my mother had to mention that was a bad omen. It took everything I could muster not to bolt back to the car and lock myself in.

An elderly man with a slightly awkward demeanor greeted

us; he welcomed us inside and guided us into a little front room, which smelled moldy. I remember noticing a bible and thought that was odd. He promptly disappeared and then reappeared moments later with a small tray of tea. "Make sure," he said, "that you leave some liquid in the bottom of your teacup and then turn the cup around three times and make a wish." And with that he left us alone. We sat in relative silence and drank our tea, which I might add did not taste particularly good but I didn't care as I was enthralled with the whole process.

When it was my time to go, the old man came for me to take me to the kitchen as this was where I was to have my fortune told. I remember just standing in the kitchen doorway with my empty cup in my hand. Through the low lighting, my eyes spotted her, an old lady sitting at the far end of the surprisingly large room.

"Come in," she said, as I approached her table where many had shared their problems in life. The silence was awkward and I was secretly afraid she was going to tell me she couldn't read my tealeaves because I was young, but just as afraid she would. I sat down across from her. She took my cup and peered into and said, "Let's see what your fate will be." Her voice cut through me like a knife, she was one who had seen through the veil, she knew what happened in shadows ... I was terrified. I watched her go to work with the skill and experience of an ancient seer; she analyzed the tea grains and poured out her wisdom. She saw multiple marriages, near death experiences, my mother's suffering and much more. I only wish I had been mature enough to heed her warnings. She did indeed see into my future that night and that early experience stayed with me and encouraged me to become a reader myself, which the old lady by the swamp had also foretold.

After that night, I read everything I could find on psychic powers, astrology and anything paranormal. I eventually became friends with a woman who did readings professionally, though instead of tealeaves she used playing cards. I persuaded her to teach me this craft, and over the next couple of years she taught me and we became great friends.

My decision to take this path seriously and make it a career choice happened on a camping trip to Northern Ontario. We had planned to camp, but after a few days on a thin mattress we'd had enough and we traded our tent for a cottage. Our home for the next week was a quaint little cabin located just a few hours north of Toronto. The view was magnificent. We were surrounded in a kaleidoscope of pristine Northern beauty. It was the ideal place to begin a new journey of spiritual awakening. For the first time in a long time, this native woman felt truly connected to Mother Earth. The tapestry of colors and rugged landscape captured my heart and when I breathed, I wanted to take all of this creative energy into me and merge with the land itself.

Walking along the worn path I could hear the echoes of the ancestors, I could sense their presence in the shadows, but I was not afraid and felt a peacefulness rise up inside of me, it was assurance that their love would guide me.

In the evenings, we'd walk down to a communal campfire and enjoy shared beverages, toasted marshmallows and good conversations.

I had bought a deck of playing cards and at the last minute I'd decided to pack them into my bag. One evening I had struck up a conversation about spiritualism with a fellow camper and the topic turned to readings. I told her I had been playing around with my card deck and she asked me if I'd give her a reading. I have to admit I was really shy about it and unsure how I would do a complete reading. But I climbed up the hill to our rustic cottage, grabbed my cards and headed back down to the fire. With a much needed cup of strong coffee, I settled myself into my comfy Muskoka chair and shuffled my cards; I decided to stick to a simple four card layout.

After the cards were pulled from the deck, I took a deep

cleansing breath and decided to just feel the cards and her together. I had picked up on people's energies before and I wanted to see if I could just tap into that ability again. It was especially easy to get into the mood, sitting near a campfire, smelling the aromas of the crackling wood, and under a canopy of stars, the energy seemed to flow effortlessly and the connectivity to spirit was felt.

At the end of the hour-long reading, she pulled some money from her wallet and handed me some cash. I refused it, but she was adamant about it and made me take the money. She insisted I was correct about everything and she felt much better about things. Everything I shared with her is what she had desired to do all along and she felt the reading was going to help make some transitions go more smoothly.

I felt really happy for her and I felt that this is what I wanted to do. I really enjoyed connecting with people and sharing with them, and so on that Northern summer night my journey into psychic development seriously began.

Weeks later on warm September day, I parked my car just down the street from a spiritualist church, and with my feet swishing through a blanket of autumn leaves, I made my way to the little white church. I had no idea what to expect, but I was pleasantly surprised to see rather ordinary looking people inside. The service was pleasant and except for the mediumship performed at the end of the service, it seemed to me like a traditional Protestant service. That would have been okay but I have never liked church services. I listened to the parishioners recite the spiritualist creed, which centers on such things as personal responsibility, the existence of God and life after death. I continued to attend the occasional service and I did attend their psychic development classes, which were very enlightening and helpful. I found that I could agree with their beliefs but my spiritual path was a Native American/Celtic path and the religious ceremonies of the spiritual churches didn't fulfill me.

My mother had been my mentor and my spiritual teacher, since we had a long time ago chosen to live far from our community. After her death I was on my own walking a familiar pagan path that was now different.

I knew that the foundation of my beliefs could not change, that is why I didn't connect with the services at the spiritualist church.

As an aboriginal woman, I feel a strong connection to this land … to nature. As a Métis person, my heritage gives me a distinct way of bringing two powerful cultures together, the Cree and the Celtic, and it is from the merging of these two flames of spiritual knowledge that are so similar and so powerful that sustain me with a deep and profound inner peace.

In reality all our paths lead us back to a common circle … the Sacred Hoop … everything has spirit and everything is sacred, Awen.

When I tap into spirit, I am consciously linking with the energies of the Sacred Hoop that we are all part of; the elements, the stone people, the plant people, the swimmers, the winged ones the four legged and the two legged, creepers and crawlers. It is the energy of all creation that holds us together. Deep inside us, we are all one, and that is why when we open our minds and feel with our hearts, we become aware of the relationship we have with each other and our world.

When developing, it is important to be curious and open but it is also necessary to be protective and cautious, many people believe there is no evil, but I seriously doubt you'd find any aboriginal culture on this planet that doesn't acknowledge there is such a thing as darkness.

Even when I deal with dark people, and I have dealt with my share of them voluntarily and involuntarily, while I do not consider those dark people sacred, there is a purpose for them or they would not be here, the lessons that they have taught me are sacred because they have helped me gain wisdom.

Walking in the higher vibrations of gratitude, love and harmony is your best defence against negative energies.

We are more than our physical bodies, we are spiritual beings and if we tap into our true essence, we can remove the blocks in our lives. With divination, we can access our spiritual side for counsel in order to make better choices about the future. Consulting our inner selves by way of oracle cards, we can put an end to confusion and gain a renewed optimism to move forward in our lives with confidence. This method of renewing hope and bringing insight to situations is what healing divination is all about.

There is a very sacred side to readings, you will connect with people emotionally, spirituality and mentally, in a manner that is very pure and honest. There are realizations that go on in a half an hour reading, there are connections that people will remember for the rest of their lives and connections I will remember for the rest of my life.

Enjoy this journey you are about to embark on, as I can guarantee that you are going to meet some fantastic people. You will be shocked, frightened, intrigued, and discover things about yourself you never knew. You will cry, laugh, and eventually you will discover if you really like people or not. If you realize you don't like connecting with people, walk away from this path now. But if you really enjoy meeting people and connecting with them, then carry on in the Creator's name and enjoy the discovery. It is a beautiful dream to aspire to be a healer and through the immeasurable mysteries of existence, we come to learn who we truly are.

Chapter 2

Purification, Prayer & Protection

Mother Earth, disperse the darkness and heal my soul...
Morning whispers with the promise of a new day, the smell of
the herbs smoldering in my shell, are the perfumes of Mother
Earth. I spark my match and light my herbs, and with a deep
breath, I breathe in the sweet musky smoke of these trusted
friends. Cupping my hands together, I bring the smokiness up
and around my head and shoulders and then swoosh it towards
my legs and feet. Finally, I bring the smoke to my chest/heart and
I bring in the spirit of the Earth.

My family taught me that before I perform any intuitive work
I must be cleared and cleansed of any negative vibrations. In
order to cleanse your energy you need to enter into a state of
gratitude and forgiveness: gratitude releases blockages and
opens the gates of abundance, so before you pray and smudge,
place your mind set in a state of thankfulness.

Purification is important. It helps us to release toxins that
have accumulated in our aura; collections of negative energies
that are being held within our energy field. These pools of detrimental vibrations can be memories, actions and emotions from
this lifetime and prior incarnations. That is why it is not enough
to just waft smoke around our bodies, we should be connecting
to the plant that is being used in the smudging ritual, and ask
that plant being for healing.

For example, sage is an ancient healer and an empowering
presence in spiritual work. I would say it is essential to have this
plant being as a helpmate.

When we smudge, we lift the doorway into the spiritual
realm. Once the herbs are ignited, there is power and strength,
and that which illuminates our prayers, hangs thick in the air as

it swirls and twirls around our heads. Whether by morn or starlight the smoke will surely rise with steady ease — beauty and love ascending upwards towards the divine, and the trust is there between sage and human. I gaze upwards to an azure sky; I want the universe to accept my offerings. The song of the sage resonating through the air and fills me with awe and wonder ... is this healing? ... I think so.

Let us say you are about to cleanse yourself with rosemary. This plant helps increase psychic awareness and is excellent to use before any kind of divination work. At first, I go through the series of meditations of tuning into what gender it is, and what kind of personality it has, just so I can get a foothold of the plants vibration. While I am holding the dried rosemary, I let my mind relax, let the scent of it come to me, and then I take a deep breath as if I am taking the energy of this plant into my lungs. Relaxing my mind, I put out my psychic sensors towards the rosemary "feeling" not "assuming", remember there is a huge difference in those intentions one is intuitive the last one is not. So before I place the herb in my smudging bowl, I imagine the smoke from the rosemary drifting around my head and I "feel" what the energy of that smoke is like and how it affects me. I allow the vibration of the rosemary smoke to heal and to communicate with me. Once I have made the psychic connection with the rosemary, with much respect I ask for healing, wisdom and protection.

I sometimes get a sense with rosemary that it doesn't want to work through burning, but in the water element. I will add the herb to a spray bottle and spritz it around my body, making sure I get the front, sides and back of myself.

Warm and musky frankincense expects to be burned. This resin has an inner knowing of its duty of warding off evil and cleansing people and places. Frankincense is a mighty shield from evil because it knows how evil thinks and behaves, and so it can always outsmart it. Its energy is sharp and direct and nothing negative can withstand its force.

Sometimes we do not know how to pray, when this happens it is a good idea to light some incense and meditate. Resins such as frankincense and myrrh know the mysteries of the divine and can help us in our intimate moments with our God.

Cleansing the energy around the body using the smoke from burning materials such as frankincense, tobacco and sage, is called smudging. Not all plants should be inhaled so do your research about what is okay to smudge with and what is not. I have listed a few resins and herbs at the end of this chapter that I use in my spiritual path.

There are a few methods of working with plants to cleanse your energy field and your environment. You can add some petals or leaves to container of water, if I am doing this I only make a small quantity because the water can go rancid. Most of the time if I want to use a spray I will add some essential oils to the water such as rosemary or sweet grass oil and a couple of drops of witch hazel. One of my favorite smudging mixtures for the spray bottle is lavender and amber, the scent of these two combined is beautiful and I find that the lavender gives me strength and helps me speak my truth without fear. The amber oil teaches me to not spill my beans too quickly and above all to always be discreet, so you see there's a beautiful balance between these two energies, not just in spiritual truths but in fragrance as well.

The oils sprayed around yourself and the room before a reading or any psychic work creates an atmosphere of balance. From my research, I have found that using one teaspoon of vodka or witch hazel in a small bottle filled with water, and five to ten drops of an essential oil work fine for me. But I suggest that you read up on essential oils and speak to an aromatherapist if you'd like to use them for cleansing and protection. Remember never spray into your face.

I love to bathe myself in the aromas of an herb, resin or spice.

Smoke is so mysterious; it stealthily encircles things. It's as if I'm being enclosed in a cloud ethereal bliss ... soothing protection from our Earth Mother. I have unquestionably discovered that smudging shifts the vibration of my mood from stressful to being peaceful.

Why is it important to smudge and to connect with plant beings? It is because plants are alive, they have intelligence and the Creator gifted them with the ability to heal us. Many people have animal totems, and like myself and for no real particular reason, some people are more inclined to connect with the plant kingdom.

For example if you have depression you might take St John's Wort, or if you had trouble sleeping you'd drink some chamomile tea and if you need a prayer partner you might consider tobacco. In my book *Walking the Path: The Cree to the Celtic,* I have rituals that help you find your plant totem and rituals to bring those energies to you.

I have my own journal that I keep, and within it are some of the herbs, resins and oils that I have smudged with, and how the plants affected me.

Try if you can to find a picture of an herb you'd like to smudge with, for example let say you'd like to incorporate nutmeg incense into your collection. Find a picture of nutmeg and just look at it for a while, relax your mind and "feel" what gender is it, what type of personality it has. Imagine yourself eating nutmeg, see the nutmeg energy as sparkles and watch it as it enters your body. Where does it seem to flow to in your body? What does it want to do inside the body? For example, when I tune into nutmeg I see it in its raw state, I imagine I am breathing it in. I feel its energies all around me, and in my mind's eye, I see it in my mouth and going down my throat. Then I let go, I let it flow and I watch the sparkles of the nutmeg take my focus where they desire to go to in my body. I hear the word "heart" and I feel the energy of the nutmeg and see it flowing to my heart and through my bloodstream. Next, I focus on my arms and legs and I have a sensation of warming. Later I will research about the benefits of nutmeg on the body and perhaps I'd discover that my meditation was right and add some nutmeg to dishes, soups and my journal.

Now visualize burning the nutmeg, focus your attention on the smoke and ask what kind of vibration it has and how will it help you and the energy of a space. Picture the smoke wafting around your body and ask how it may change your energy. Ask yourself these questions and always do this before allowing an item to affect your aura. This exercise is important because certain Earth Teachers bring benefits, such as strength from daisy, love from rose, joy from apple. As a smudging tool, you can burn dried apple and orange peel, which are nice when mixed with spices such as cinnamon and cloves, just always tune into them first and see if their qualities are what you need.

Let's say I am worried about something. In my mind's eye, I will imagine my smudging items laid out before me and I will ask myself what can help me feel serene and peaceful. Then I open myself up to my herbs, oils and spices, and get a general feeling of their collective energies. As I am linking to them, their vibrations will reach out towards my vibration. I close my eyes again and I will see all my smudging items laid out before me on a table, I will think "peace". At the back of my mind, I hold the need for an item to help me relax, and I link the word "peace". Then I watch and feel the herbs and resins respond to my need. I keep my focus on the items on the table and slowly I am drawn to one of them, it becomes denser in my inner vision I open my eyes and I find it is lavender. I will connect with lavender through my thoughts and feelings, the aim is to listen and feel the plant.

There are some ways you can experience how the plant or resin will affect your aura and mood without burning them. Start with selecting an herb you'd like to imagine smudging with such as lavender, and next place a picture of that item above your head or in your heart area and "feel it". Allow the energy of the plant to spread itself out into your energy field and notice the response to your body and emotions. Is this the sensation you need? Transform the material into smoke and feel the smoke around your body … psychically feel it, what is the smoke telling you, how is it helping you. If you are satisfied with the results from this meditation, the next step is to use the item in smudging.

With practice, these steps become easier and with little effort, you will know what herbs and oils are good for you. The Hallowed four for me are tobacco, sage, sweet grass and cedar. Before doing any psychic work I usually smudge myself and my area with a mixture of three of these and then afterwards I smudge myself again.

Once you get to know your plants, you will get to know them on a personal level. For example if you're feeling a bit drained and need a pick me up, you can light a charcoal tablet and place some chamomile and spearmint onto it, these two are quite capable of lifting the spirits.

It is extremely important to enjoy the aroma of items that you use to make your aura healthy and vibrate. Beautiful scents helps lower blood pressure, ease stress and anxiety and bring a general feeling of wellbeing, but in smudging as well as ritual it goes even deeper, it connects us to the moment, it connects us to the plant being. The scent of the herbs and oils resonate with our healing, they create beautiful memories, so when we smell those items, we recall serene moments that we have experienced. When developing your intuition it is really important to take the time to nurture your bodies and your spirit.

Tying together some herbs, flowers or tree boughs and swishing them around our bodies is so refreshing and grounded and nice to do after practicing psychic skills.

There are so many ways nature can heal us, even just lying on the ground and absorbing the energy of our Earth Mother can restore your sense of balance. Often after walking in the woods and I lean against a tree and ask for healing. As you become aware that everything is alive and has spirit, you will come across a tree or plant that needs healing. You should always pray for them and send them healing energy by visualizing a green glow around the plant restoring it to perfect health. If you have received a healing from any plant being, including trees, always leave a gift of such as a flower or herb.

Steps for Smudging Self and Environment

Select an herb you'd like to cleanse yourself with, break it up and place it in a fireproof container (or use it in its stick form). Light it preferably with matches because they are natural compared to a lighter, which is not. Allow the smoke to surround yourself, object or area. If you are smudging yourself, cup the smoke and bring it over your head and to your heart and then direct it to your lower body. When you breathe in the smoke from the smudge, you breathe in your Mother and when you wash the smoke over your body, you are washing in Mother Earth's beauty. It is our privilege to love and to cherish her. When you smudge, raise your herbs to the Creator and Mother Earth and give thanks to them, and give thanks to the Earth Teachers and the Spirit Helpers.

Do the same if you are smudging an object, allow the smoke to encircle it completely and pray while you are cleansing it. If you are performing a cleansing for a space, do so in a clockwise direction and make sure you smudge all the corners and closets and pay extra attention to places where there has been any reported negativity. When finished always dispose of the ashes outside in nature such as by a tree or garden.

Cleansing an Area and Raising its Vibration

Color is not just the pigment in paint, it is energy and it can affect our moods and the vibration of our surroundings. If you are dealing with an environment for whatever reason feels unhealthy, you can be sure it is because of human activity that has left an imprint on the land or building.

Using color is one method of healing a place or a person. When you think of it, we are light, our spirits are energies that remit light, and the shades of our auras are affected by our emotions and our experiences. Actions and thoughts are energy and those energies produce a color. A psychic can enter a place where there has been violence or arguing and sense and see the negativity as pools of dark colors. My suggestion for cleansing an area or person is to first perform a smudging ritual, followed by placing crystals around the area. If you are cleansing a person, have the person carry some crystals that have been attuned to healing, and then visualize the place or person saturated in a color.

Program a crystal by smudging it and holding it to your heart or forehead and ask the crystal to work for healing, repeat the words until you feel it has sunk into your crystal.

Something to Consider for Yourself and a Client

Herbs as Talismans

When doing readings, or just for everyday, if you feel you need it, you can create a sachet of herbs to wear on your body. Fill a sachet with dried herbs, which you have prayed over and asked for protection. You can also have a dish of dried herbs on a table beside you when doing readings for added protection.

If I am using a spice to smudge an area with, such as cinnamon, as you rub some of the incense together, concentrate on the intention of what you wish to achieve with it. I suggest using frankincense, sandalwood chips, dried apples or orange peel, to bind with the spice.

Herbs, Resins, Oils and Spices for Healing

Cinnamon, frankincense, sandalwood oil and sandalwood chips, are great for binding with spices. Dried citrus peel is great too as are myrrh, benzoin, cloves, lavender, juniper, sage and tobacco. I don't use sweet grass to protect, though I will use this to attract good spirits and the same with rose petals, which are very good for bringing in angelic help. Cedar is best for purifying larger areas, but can be used on people as well. Dragon's blood is very powerful and excellent for divination work.

Smudging, prayer, and ceremony, can all bring in healing and protection, but you must remember to be prudent in your own spiritual and physical health and wellbeing. My advice is to never channel spirit, in my opinion, channeling is not working intuitively and it is not developing your psychic abilities. I do not believe that a being of a higher vibration, such as an angel, can lower theirs to step into our bodies and why would they? We are here to learn and to grow on our own.

Automatic writing is another form of channeling and in my mind extremely dangerous, as is holding a séance. There are many discarnate beings who roam the earth who are only too eager to find a host to inhabit and drain of them of their life force, so beware, don't be full of fear but be mature and responsible about your development. I have been on the path of learning to be intuitive for many years and I have never channeled as it is dangerous and it is unnecessary.

Chapter 3

Angels, Guides & Totems

Guiding lights...

Slow down, take a moment ... or two, and link with the beauty of your guardian angel. Allow your mind and body to melt into the arms of a celestial being of pure loving energy, listen to their gentle lullaby and let all your worries slip from your mind and body. Now imagine breezy swirls of pretty pastel colors twirling about you, bringing you warmth and healing and know that each color is being given to you from an angel and each color is revitalizing your being.

Angels can show you how to enter into the depths of quiet reflections, and with awareness of breath and visualizations, find that inner calmness. Angel medicine is intuitive and is inspiration for wellness and peaceful thoughts, mediating with angel energy will heighten your vibration and bring you to a whole new level of intuitive abilities.

The purpose of your guide or angel is to assist you in learning your lessons and keep you on track, so that you can embrace your life's purpose. Spirit guides and angels use our conscious and unconscious minds to communicate with us. Guardian angels, power animals and guides, make our lives so much easier because they can see the real cause of our blocks, and when we take the time to listen to our inner self, we can hear their advice. Get into a receptive mood by smudging, lighting a candle and make an offering such as frankincense and myrrh to your guide and guardian angel.

Meditation is not the only way to increase your vibrations, ritual does the same thing, and so performing simple acts such as praying, lighting candles and making an offering, cleanses and purifies you and your environment, and encourages the spiritual beings to draw closer.

I feel angels have a deep connection to us and I believe that some angels have been human in another lifetime, but their lives were full of service to others and therefore they evolved and eventually became angels. Over the years of doing readings, I affectionately became known as the "angel reader". I have done readings for many people, some have many angels around them, some have none and some have angels standing at a distance watching them. I can always tell the difference between a person who prays and people who don't. The people who are spiritual and live in compassion for others, have angels around them. People who are not, usually have no angels with them. People who were once spiritual and stopped or people who have others praying for them, have angels watching them sometimes at a distance, this always tells me that an angel is willing to work with them, but the person hasn't opened up to their angelic energies yet. Working with angels, I have come to know some angel energies by the color and feel of them. Archangel Raphael is always jewel tones, while Archangel Gabriel is bright yellow.

The bible teaches that an angel is a pure spirit created by God; the word angel comes from the Greek word *angelos,* which means messenger. Scriptures give us no indication of when angels were created. Pseudo-Dionysius the Areopagite wrote about the nine orders of angels — Angels, Archangels, Virtues, Thrones, Principalities, Powers, Dominions, Seraphim, and Cherubim

According to Catholicism, angels carry out God's missions on earth, such as the Annunciation where Archangel Gabriel came and asked Mary to be the mother of God. We are taught in Christianity that just like us, angels are creations of God, but unlike us, they did not need time and reflection to grow in God's wisdom and they were never human.

I on the other hand have a different take on angels, I believe they come from another dimension, they exist at a higher vibration, they have their own society and they have do have a providence for humankind.

I see many angels that look like roman warriors, while my youngest son Ben says he has seen angels with long robes and symbols on their chest, and that some of those symbols look similar to our symbols for the elements. He felt their work is mostly centered on nature. Ben first saw these beings when I took him to a place where I pray and perform ceremony; he remarked that my ceremonies attracted them to that area.

Bonds of Love That Can Never Be Broken

It is my belief that Guardian angels are assigned to human souls and non-human souls as well, such as animals. If we have called on or attracted an angel they never leave our side, they understand our nature and they are here to help us fulfill our divine mission.

In contacting your guardian angel, select a time when you are not tired and a time of day when it is quiet. Mentally ask your angel to come forth. In your mind's eye, you see a glowing light, now ask your angel to surround you in the loving light of God. This color could be white or any other color, but it will never be black or grey. If an angel appears to me in tones of greens and blues, I know those are my healing colors and I try to surround myself in those shades of color.

Your angel can make themselves known to you in another form, such as an animal or bird, just allow it to happen. Greet your angel by saying, *God bless you*, or *May the God and Goddess bless you*. Give thanks to your angel for all the time they have helped you and protected you. Allow messages to come to you and be open to guidance.

Feelings of love, warmth, hope and inspiration, are the feelings of angelic contact.

A spiritual guide is a being who has experienced life on this planet and is aware of how life in this dimension works. He has agreed to work with his ward in helping this person to achieve what they set out to learn and accomplish. Guides are spiritual beings who have spent a fair amount of time in spirit, and so have knowledge not only of this earthly plane but also of the spiritual plane. This is necessary, because guides, like angels, have to protect us and have to know how to guide us. A guide can be someone we have known from a previous life or a family member a friend or a lover. They are other spirits that we have forged a strong bond with, it is a bond that has been tested by trials, tribulations even hatred, yet the sacred connection still survives, in fact thrives.

Guides, like angels, will always give us feelings of love and encouragement and they would never be abusive. Just like when you desire to contact your angel, you can also learn to be more aware of the spirits who help you. One method I practice to enable me to see my guides, is to sit quietly for a while, relax my mind and ask my guides to come forward, just like in the angel meditation. If I have a hard time seeing what comes forward, I will go and stand in front of a mirror. Relaxing my mind to that state of just below consciousness, I think to myself ... I know there are beings of love and beauty around me. I ask God to allow me to see my guardian spirits who are with me. I stare into the mirror of the space around me and I allow images to form either in my mind, or in the reflection of the mirror. I don't actually see them in the physical, I see them in my mind's eye in the reflection of the mirror standing behind me. It takes practice, but I have found this method very useful in seeing spirit around me.

We are Pure Spirit in a Human Body

An elder of the Star Beings hugs me tightly, and then placing his hands on my shoulders says, " Remember to allow your spirit to guide you, for soon you will forget this place. You must in a way unlearn all that you have learned so you can learn anew. You have performed the Anam Cara ritual. You know Wolf will be there to guide you."

Tears cloud his eyes and he quickly kisses my cheek then whispers, "You are loved."

I watch him grow smaller as I float away from him. There is such tremendous sadness leaving this place where love happens so effortlessly, the place I am descending to is dangerous and I will need all my wits about me. Suddenly an arm comes around my waist and I am drawn closer to my guide ... Wolf.

In his steady and unwavering presence, he reassures me that I have prepared myself for this: "The wisdom of the Cosmos lies within you," he says. Wolf bends his head and whispers to me, "We embark on this journey together, we are forged in love and I will never forsake you."

I breathe a sigh of relief and allow my head to rest on his chest. The story of our bond is in the memories of the battles we have fought together. One last time I grasp his hand and say, "Promise me that when I am still, you will speak to me."

He answers, "I will."

With trembling lips, I softly say to him, "Promise to keep me warm, safe and strong."

He replies, "I will."

With a false expression of bravery, I turn to him and say, "I'll keep you in my heart." With those words I let go of his hand. I am born.

Trust Me as I Trust You

Anam Cara in Celtic spirituality means soul friend, companion or guide. It is the gift of love and trust that two souls share with each other. Each one balances the other; the bond is holy and sacred.

We are here on terms of sacred contracts. We all must do our share in helping humanity to advance. Every one of us is here for a reason, together we can heal humanity and to try to fix the damage that has been done to our Earth Mother.

Each of us is a manifestation of the energy that is the circle of life or the sometimes named sacred hoop. What this means is that each of us are on journeys: we are born, we have relationships, we have families, we then pass the torch onto the next generation and die only to be reborn again and the cycle continues. We see this cycle in the world all around us from nature to the phases of the moon.

The Sacred Circle of which we are bound, is the web of life, and it connects us all and allows us to freely share our knowledge with each other. In order to know our path, it is extremely important to consciously establish the connection to that web, which is the intelligence of all creation, and therefore it is wise to keep oneself in balance, so that with a clear mind we begin to know and to trust in our own inner wisdom.

Each of us carries a fire within; we need to tend to our fire so that we can maintain our health and well-being. Our ancestors were gifted with knowledge of how to heal. Their sufferings were not in vain, for it is through their wisdom and their love that we can attain wellness.

I think there are many opinions on the subject of spiritual helpers or guides, many believe that everyone has a guide at birth and I tend to disagree with that statement. From what I have seen clairvoyantly and from what I have learned in prayer and meditation is that not all come in with help. These beings are gifts and we are gifts to them, there is a beautiful exchange between one and another. Depending on where a person is on their spiritual development, we can trade with each other. What I mean is one time I can act as a guide to my guide and vice versa. I don't think it is often that one guide knows a whole lot more than their ward. I think there is a balance between the two, they are helping each other, and they work as a unit.

My family taught me that there are many beings that can guide us and help us and not all are human souls. But I believe that sometimes even non-human souls can present themselves as people and I think they do this in order to make us feel more comfortable.

Guides are linked to our souls and so have complete access to our thoughts and can speak to us freely through gut feelings, hunches and premonitions, and so yes, our spirits do guide us but our spiritual helpers are linked spiritually with us so it is one fined tuned working unit. I think it gets confusing when you watch famous psychics on TV that seem to channel their guides personality, it leads many people to believe that you should channel your guide. I don't believe this is true in fact I think it's unnecessary

Spirit guides help us problem solve, but they remain in the background watching us and encouraging us with words of wisdom. We hear them through our thoughts and dreams.

Totems or power animals can be with us at birth or we can perform ritual to attract them to us. In my book *Walking the Path: The Cree to the Celtic,* I have ceremonies that honor totems and bring them into our lives. A totem animal can give us strength and courage even when we think we have none. Pay attention to dreams, for often power animals or totem animals speak to us through our unconscious minds. When we are attracted to an animal, notice the traits of those creatures for they can lend some of their natural abilities to us.

Always ask the Divine to bless your angels, guides and totems and bless the connection between you and them.

Chapter 4

Angel Medicine

Joy is meditation...

Slow down, take a moment or two, and link with the beauty of your guardian angel. Allow your mind and body to melt into the arms of a celestial being of pure loving energy. Listen to their gentle lullaby and let all your worries slip from your mind and body.

Now imagine breezy swirls of pastel colors twirling about you, bringing you warmth and healing and know that each color is being given to you from an angel and each color is revitalizing your being.

Angels can show you how to enter into the depths of quiet reflections, and with awareness of breath and visualizations, find that inner calmness. Angel medicine is intuitive and is inspiration for wellness and peaceful thoughts.

Angels of our Earth Mother, teach us how to heal from many types of trauma. Meditation is a tool that is often used in healing. The merging of angel medicine and meditation creates an ideal atmosphere to heal. It also creates a harmonizing energy to grow intuitive abilities. It is believed that angels can work as guides. They can be a link to other spiritual dimensions. Angels are very protective and have been known to help humans who are in danger. They can also act as wise guides when working with finer energies.

Meditating with angels is a process of deep relaxation and visualization, which leads to states of consciousness that brings serenity, blissfulness and healing.

One of the beauties of this act of self-love is a profound state of deep relaxation or restful state. Meditation helps us focus and improves our abilities to be attentive even outside of the meditative state. Meditation helps stop the constant chatter in our minds and helps to break down the blockages that we have built and can give us a sense of control over our lives.

Making time to meditate helps us to connect with our spiritual selves; the realization happens where we discover our own divinity — I am love, I love and I am loved.

Meditation, when practiced regularly, can help release the chains of a soul that is aching to fly high above the clouds, psychic overload and the pain in our bodies. Solitude, quietening of the mind, slowing down, making a sacred vow to have reverence for your spirit and the spirits of all living things, and to be mindful of your sacred contract with the Creator and our Earth Mother, is a way of accepting who we are and our place in the sacred hoop of which we are part.

There is no overnight path to becoming good at meditation it takes dedication and practice. Meditation is an important component in psychic development because it opens a passageway into your own inner consciousness, resulting in enhanced awareness of self and other forms of energies and vibrations.

Energy permeates everything; it is within everyone and connects everyone and everything together. This is why we can sense emotions and receive visions off objects, such as in the skill of psychometry. Energy leaves an imprint in reality. Vibration is the different frequency that energy is at such as properties of density, flow and color. Empaths like me feel those energies and are sensitive of them constantly.

Awareness of other people's varying forms of energy and their vibrations is what being intuitive all is about. In this book, the hoped for result of meditation is for enhancement of psychic ability, controlling the onslaught of emotional baggage that an empath can experience, understanding your inner voice and trusting your initial responses to information picked up on items and living beings ... getting the feel of energy and vibrations.

Quiet Minds and Hearts

Learning to be psychic is all about connecting your heart intelligence with your head intelligence and recognizing energy patterns such as knowing when energy shifts, whether is it blocked or free flowing, is low or high, and is healthy or tainted. If the mind is not used to being quiet, it is impossible to get into the practice of performing these processes. Feeling vibrations of energy can be achieved with a relaxed mind ... a quiet mind; peaceful thoughts produce a serene heart, so practice peacefulness.

We are flashes of celestial flames; glowing, connecting, karmic rays of radiant light. Our destiny is to love and to learn without shame. Meditation is a beacon that illuminates the darkness and brings us back on our paths, so when our minds reconnect with the celestial ember that burns inside us, the result is our intuition blossoms and develops, we are not suppose to remain ignorant of our own abilities.

The Universe Listens

It is so important to be in a state where you can listen. The act of listening is so imperative to our development as listening is an important aspect of communication. What most of us are unaware of is that spirits listen to our thoughts and words. In silence they are learning and progressing sometimes through our experiences. In the practice of meditation, you can be detached to messages, visions and thoughts that drift into your consciousness. Sensations can roll through you, allow them to come, but remember you can chose to let them go. If you wish to let certain feelings go, then imagine a beautiful blue wave of the purest water sweeping all negativity away leaving you refreshed. For years I experienced a heightened sensitivity to my environment because I could feel other people's feelings, and with the discomfort of a chronic disease such as fibromyalgia, it just intensified everything.

I really needed ways to manage being an empath and being ill at the same time. Meditation was the key to being able to cope with being sensitive and living with a chronic illness, that is not to say that I don't have my dark days but they are fewer and I can cope easier.

The word "meditation" means many different things to many different people. I practice different forms of meditation but the aim is to be mindful, quiet and aware. Mindfulness is a type of meditation that brings our attention to the present, to be mindful of our thoughts, keeping them on the present and to anything that his happening inside us or around us. There is a meditation, which I refer to as Angel Healing, here are a few examples of this meditation:

Healing Meditation Exercise, With Angels

Anoint yourself...

Take 2 tablespoons of olive oil or grapeseed oil and into it place a couple of drops of lavender or chamomile essential oil. Stir it with a wooden spoon or finger. At this point I will place the word "healing" or the word "angel" over the oil. I will then anoint my forehead and chest bone with a small dab of oil.

Always dilute the essential oil before using it on yourself and always make sure if the oil is safe to be applied to skin.

Sit down and make yourself comfortable, the smell of the essential oils is to help calm your mind and bring you into a relaxed state so you can meditate with the angels. Perform some deep breaths and then begin your prayers to the angels.

Angel of Water I invoke thee and I embrace the gift of healing you bring to me.

Focus on your saliva and imagine it is balanced and pure and it feels like a lightly salty ocean of goodness. Now imagine the fluid is in your eyes and is pure and sparkling. Now take that pleasant sensation and move it through the fluid around your brain and down into your spinal column. Move it throughout your bloodstream and then through all the water of your body.

Angel of Earth I invoke thee and I embrace the gift of healing that comes from thee.

Imagine the strength from Mother Earth feeding all your bones, teeth and cartilages in your body. Visualize the Angel of Earth regenerating your body and bringing your being into a state of wellness.

Angel of Air I invoke thee and I embrace the gift of healing that comes from thee.

With eyes closed, turn your attention to your breathing, breathe normally and become aware of the air entering your nostrils and traveling down to your lungs. Imagine that each particle of air is like a sparking diamond filling every cell in your body with healing.

Your mantra is: *Angel of air healing me.*

Angel of Fire I invoke thee and I embrace the gift of healing that comes from thee.

This meditation was a gift to me from the angels and I use it when I feel I am being attacked or sickly. I imagine a beautiful blue flame purifying my energy field, purifying my body, burning away all sickness and negativity.

Mantra: *Angel of the blue flame I thank thee.* (I will use the blue flame if I believe I am being psychically attacked).

During a meditative walk, I am not withdrawing from the outside world as I must be aware of where I am walking or else I could get hurt. I focus on my feet and the ground and the sensations of walking. I find myself even more aware of my body when I walk as to when I'm sitting mediating; all the while I am mindful of the sun, wind and the sounds of nature. Sometimes I go on a meditative walk around my neighborhood, I am mindful of the light cast by the streetlamps for it chases away the darkness and just like angels they guide me home.

During a meditative walk, I am mindful of the spirits that are with me; guardian angels and ancestors that I may not see with my eyes, but are with me in my heart. Friendships don't depend on sight and sound, there are bonds that last forever and our guides are sent from heaven to walk us through the steps of lessons.

Anam Cara: Soul Friend

Relaxing Meditation

Take a deep breath in and exhale slowly. Do this a couple of times and then relax your shoulders and arms and let all the tension drain from your jaw and neck. Be sure to relax your face. Relax your chest and stomach muscles and then your legs and imagine all the stress exiting your body through your toes and fingers. Imagine a perfect sphere of creamy light inside your head and move that sphere down through your neck. Move the ball of light right down through your body and allow it to pool like a golden puddle of creamy liquid at your feet.

Count from one to ten and then start again and count from one to ten again, do this a few times and then say a mantra in your head such as:

Angel of Love, soak me in your beauty and light.

Allow feelings of love to fill your whole being and then open your eyes and take a couple of deep breaths; wiggle your toes and open your eyes feeling grounded and refreshed.

Meditation, when practiced regularly, can help release the chains of a soul that is aching to fly high above the clouds, psychic overload, and the pain in our bodies. Solitude, quietening the mind, slowing down making a sacred vow to have reverence for your spirit and the spirits of all living things, and to be mindful of your sacred contract with the Creator and our Earth Mother, is a way of accepting who we are, in our present.

Awareness of other people's varying forms of energy and their vibrations is what being intuitive all is about. In this book, the hoped for result of meditation, is for enhancement of psychic ability.

Meditation for Recognizing Various Vibrations of Energy

Take a deep breath in, relax your body, relax your mind and imagine a beautiful summer garden of various flowers. The earth is lush and green, FEEL how fertile it is; how alive it is. Now be aware of the flowers how they are swaying softly in a summer breeze, FEEL the softness of the summer air. Reds, blues, yellows, imagine each flower, FEEL their color, FEEL their fragrance and FEEL the vibration of each flower's personality. When you have finished cover yourself in a beautiful cascading shower of white and golden light, take a deep breath in and relax.

Chapter 5

Deer Medicine

Intuition, Ego and Instinct...

My mother taught me that from an Indian's perspective, medicine is about restoring a whole person and not about curing a specific disease. That is why relationships with all of nature are so important and necessary for health and wellbeing. In this chapter, I will discuss deer medicine and what my family taught me about it.

The spirit of the deer is medicine for me. When I burn my sweet grass, my heart is softened for my friend the deer. The medicine this creature brings is peacefulness, patience and a heightened sense intuition. It is an omen that it is time to go within, do not fear and do not fight the direction that the Creator is taking you in. Deer people understand the difference between intuition, ego and instinct. So that when life is dark, the spirit of the deer will guide you through the forest. The strength and beauty of this spirit animal is the balance between intuition, ego and instinct.

Intuition is our friend that guides us through life; it allows us to live peaceful and stable lives. Our heart's intelligence, our gut feelings are our layers of protection. When we listen to our hearts, we glow with the Creator's wisdom. I can assure you that from the moment your consciousness was formed you were intuitive to some degree. Just as we all have our own unique appearances and our unique personalities, we have our own unique style of being intuitive and our own way of connecting with our own inner spirit, that is what being psychic all is about.

Living and being guided by our inner wisdom, our intuition helps us to live balanced lives. Information is all around us, our bodies are powerful transmitters and receivers, when we become aware of influences and energies through intuition, the information becomes useful.

My Métis ethnicity is also a spiritual path. The root of my spirituality is in my heart, prayers are said with the heart and they are carried by the winds to my ancestors. My ancestors' gift to me is wisdom and understanding, the awareness of knowing life is more than the physical, and that true awareness happens when I am living through the intelligence of my heart. The fruit of this is an intuitive lifestyle. Living intuitively means you are open to guidance, you expect to receive guidance, you trust in your own intuitive guidance and you act on your intuition.

Working with totem animals and plants can help us to live in like-mindedness with the spirit of the earth. Totems or power animals can also aid us in connecting with our ancestors. In this chapter, I would like to share how all my relatives, everything seen and unseen, help me to know myself and to be connected to the world around me. This process of becoming aware of and being in tune with nature and the rhythms of the seasons, has enhanced communication between my conscious mind and my higher self and therefore the to the web of life that we are all part of. Our relatives, including the plant and rock people, look beyond appearance to see who we really are, they accept us as we are and most of the time they are willing to work with us. This ability makes them superior healers, connecting with a being of nature can help us to relax and take a journey within ourselves. Nature was the religion of the ancient Celts and as with Native Americans, both would go off to be alone in nature to be healed and renewed. I'm sure during that time alone they would discover much about who they were and their purpose in the sacred hoop of life.

Learning who we are should be our first step and one that needs to begin, because it only makes sense that before we can learn how to intuitively connect with others, we need to connect intuitively to our higher selves. Opening up psychically can be life changing and we need to be grounded in who we are spirituality and what we believe about ourselves. Many of us are taught that religion is the only way and that one must believe in a certain dogma or else face eternal damnation. Be honest with yourself, do you believe this? Or are you truly willing to explore what spirituality is without the restraints of religion? Becoming intuitive is also becoming self aware, getting to know yourself and what you want, and how fast you'd like to grow as a psychic. The more you know about yourself, the more confidence you will have in your connections with others. The more you accept yourself, the more you will be accepting of others. Society, family, friends and religion have put labels on us; we have been conditioned to hold certain beliefs about who we are, when in fact it is highly likely that it is not us at all. Part of awareness is the journey within, and since going on a vision quest can be impractical for many, including myself, we can still find those moments of solitude to drum, meditate and make offerings. We can slow down and experience those *ahh* moments. You don't have to go into the desert or have a shaman with you to connect with the Great Spirit; all you need is time alone.

Spending quality time in nature is balancing the natural world, and this anchors us in the present and brings us down to earth.

Make that time to watch the sun sink its way towards an evening sky, take in the blaze of colors that bleeds across the Creator's canvas … be far removed from the mundane and surrender yourself to the moment.

A walking meditation is taking time to meditate on the divine, nature and yourself. Our lives would be happier if we made the conscious effort to live with dignity for ourselves and all our relatives, in nature. We are valuable to the Creator and to our Earth Mother.

When we become seekers of awareness, intuition and understanding, we can experience real joy. We get out of "our heads" or "mundane thoughts". A walk in the park is an opportunity to link with a tree or to experience how a blue jay is feeling.

Be still within yourself, don't think of the kids, your partner, pets, what to pick up at the grocery store and don't feel guilty about making time for yourself. After all this is your life experience and it is not about taking care of others all the time. Making time for spiritual walks or sitting quietly and relaxing your mind is a way of life. It involves getting off the fast track of *I need to be everything to everybody all the time* mode. You cannot become aware if you're focused on others, yes the kids need to be taken care of and the bills need to be paid, but without sacred moments how can you replenish your spirit, mind and body, and without balance you could become ill and then not be able to take care of anyone.

When I am getting ready to go out for a walking meditation there are a few things that I enjoy doing first. Following a smudging with prayer, I will gather some items that are sacred to me such as a crystal or feather, something that is spirituality significant to me. These items are what some call fetishes, although I really never use that term, instead I call them an amulet because their vibrations and energy act as a protection.

My eldest son suffered a mental breakdown a few years ago, he knew he had to get out of Toronto but was unsure of where to go. He kept listening to his ego. Because of his success in life, he felt that he should be working in a certain kind of place and making a certain amount of money, but his instincts and his intuition were telling him a totally different message. He turned to his family for help and support and I tried to guide him and give him suggestions, but he couldn't get past what he thought was owed to him.

I believe he downshifted and went into survival mode what is commonly called the fight or flight response. He packed up his apartment and within weeks left Toronto for another city with little or no thought of the decision he was making. He headed there with no family, no friends and where the cost of living was extremely high and the job did not pay all that well. Looking back now, he can clearly see the signals that were there around his job interview but at the time, he was so frightened for his future he couldn't see or feel what to do.

I prayed and performed a ceremony for my son, asking for guidance. The deer resides in my medicine wheel or what I refer to as my "earth wheel", and one night driving back home with my son, we were discussing the seemingly hopeless situation we were facing with his new job in a new city, and it was becoming clear he couldn't live there. I was very depressed, I had asked for a sign to see if he should just move back home. The night was clear and quiet. In the distance, we could see farms lit up with Christmas lights and it was very beautiful. I came around a bend and there was my sign, a couple of deer and a fawn were on the road, the odd thing is they didn't run away they just stood there. We put the car in park and watched them for a moment. Suddenly about 20 deer surrounded us. They peeked at us through the windows and for a brief moment in time, my world was peaceful and serene.

Then silently they glided towards a forest, and the darkness of the pine trees opened up and swallowed them into its safety. It was amazing. They were so calm and unafraid. One of the deer came to my side of the window and looked into my eyes, and at that moment I knew it was all going to be okay. Weeks went by and it was okay, everything did fall into plan and my son was able to get out of his lease and he is now working at home and loves it.

When I began my journey into becoming aware and therefore becoming more insightful of what was really going on in my life, I walked closely with deer energy. Both Celts and Native Americans looked to the deer to help with hunting and survival wisdom. Before a hunt they would sometimes pray to the deer spirit for good success, and they would explain that they needed to kill to provide food and clothing for their loved ones. This intention is one of caring and respect for all and it is the path of the deer.

Deer medicine helps us to know things without using normal and rational processes. The deer gifts us with impressions and hunches, we will either be drawn to something or completely repelled by it, and this can happen in a flash or over time. The spirit of the deer hopes that humans will develop this ability so that we can use it deliberately whenever it is needed.

Your intuition speaks to you in a unique way that is yours alone, only you can become accustomed to your inner voice and you must be open to receiving guidance from your higher self. Your intuition provides you with direction, your inner voice speaks and you instinctively understand that this is truth. This is the foundation of wisdom the deer wishes you to drink from daily … your own living waters.

In days gone by, intuition was considered a gift that was bestowed on very few people, and those people were considered special, but now we know that everyone has the capacity for intuition and I believe the spirits of the deer helped bring this knowledge to humans. Intuition has many names, a gut feeling, hunch, inner knowing and heart feelings. Deer medicine tells us to slow down listen and feel situations, issues and people with our hearts.

Deer medicine is instinctual intuition and it includes other aspects of survival such as our instincts to survive and to thrive. Under the influence of the deer, we are likened to this magnificent animal. Many times we can experience deer dreams and visions, we see, hear, smell and feel, by the spirit of the deer. Listen to Earth's wind songs; give thanks for the dreams and visions. Deer beings know well how to survive and their wisdom is strong. For example, when we are being overloaded with information and responses to the issues going on in our lives, the beauty of the deer centers us, grounds us and then dissipates the chaos. Make an effort to live close to nature, it is important to experience walks after a soft rain, to gaze up at a painted sky and enjoy the coolness of a moonlit night.

Observe and learn the habits of the deer and you will be gaining knowledge of their medicine. Through deer dreams, deer medicine speaks to us about our sacred contract with Mother Earth and our lessons we came here to learn. Our instincts are important to us; they help us to avoid dangerous situations — our instincts are a gift from the Creator. The deer teaches us how to be instinctually intuitive and it is vital to balance these impulses and abilities in order for us to live to our highest good. I remember being taught in school about animal instincts and how through repeated experiences animals will react with certain predictably under a variety of circumstances. A cornered animal will fight, run or play dead, and an animal has an instinctive motivation to feed their young. Salmon swim upstream to spawn, geese fly south in winter. Animals are naturally in touch with their instinctual selves, it is often said that because of technology we humans are losing our sense of our intuitive and instinctive self.

Deer senses are very acute, they give us the clarity to comprehend what is going on in our lives and the lives of others, which I might add is a tremendous asset to acquire when tuning into others. The deer bestows upon us a sense of when to change habits, when to back off from people or issues and when to change ideas or plans. Under the vibration of this wise creature, we are able to sense danger and to understand what is truly going on and in what direction to run to for safety.

When deer crosses your path or lopes into your life, it signals a time to meditate on the lesson that is being presented to you. Or perhaps deer medicine is teaching you to be gentle on yourself, to be patient in your development and to be gentle with others. Don't rush your experiences but savor each adventure that comes as you awaken to your full intuitive self.

I noticed two types of voices or thoughts that come to me, one I believe comes from my ego and the other is the voice of my intuition. I have noticed over the years that when my heart sends me messages it creates an inner knowing that is so powerful I need never question it, but when my ego speaks, I do question it for it always comes with a tail of doubt. Actually, when my ego is working, I have noticed how tense my body feels and when my heart is speaking to me, it feels right and I feel relaxed. I learned early on that I cannot trust the message in my head more than the feelings of my heart, especially when doing readings.

It is important to have a healthy ego, a sense of self-esteem, but one must watch the ego when doing readings for yourself or others. The ego part of self has perceptions, beliefs and opinions, these must be pushed aside so that pure intuitive work comes through the self or spirit must be dominate. Remember though, a balanced ego is important. Someone who is of sound mind knows their weakness and strengths and accepts themselves for who they are and are accepting of others.

Our hearts are the center of our intuitive power, our modern society conditions us to listen to our heads or an expert or read a book, and when we do just this without listening to our hearts our world becomes smaller. When we learn to react intuitively we begin to trust ourselves, trust our inner knowing and gain confidence in who we are and we choose a path of heart wisdom; fed by deer medicine. Deer medicine always brings us the awareness of being connected to something bigger and that sense that the world is a wondrous place.

Chapter 6

Swan Medicine

Everything has a vibration...

Power animal Swan, aids in intuitive abilities and ushers in a time of psychic awakening

The Celts and the Native American people held all animals sacred and many of us still do, I honor all my relatives and I believe that studying the habitats of animals can teach me many things.

An animal totem is an important energy that a person uses to get in touch with specific qualities found within the animal, which the person needs or is lacking in their life. Winged ones, four-legged, creepers and crawlers, swimmers, rock people and plant people are helping spirits, and they are essential when working within the metaphysical realm. Animals come to us or we are drawn to them because they have a lesson to teach us or we sense that we need to learn something from them. I connect to a totem or power animal by meditating on the traits of that animal. Sometimes an animal guide will be with you for life and sometimes for just a short period of time and then be replaced by another animal or perhaps a plant being. Swan energy is very intuitive, and I have found that mediating on their beauty and sensing how they are aware of the cycles of life and the energies of Mother Earth, aids me in my intuitive pursuits.

There is a favorite park that I often walk through, which is known for its swans. This is where I first fell in love with mysterious beauty and grace of this Earth Teacher. Swan medicine inspires within me impressions of the importance of commitment, not only to family and friends, but also to my own beliefs. Swan's mixture of beauty and strength bestows strength to my body and soul. The traits of this bird teach me to be true to my nature, to heed the signs that are around me, and not to ignore my inner knowing. Swan medicine brings awareness to our lives, increases our intuitive abilities and teaches us patience and understanding.

It is my belief that clairsentience is the most common psychic gift today. Clairsentience is the ability of being sensitive or empathic, of having the ability to "sense emotions" beyond that of having sympathy.

An example of this would be sensing someone who is trying to quit smoking. You might suddenly start to crave a cigarette, whether you smoke or not. Or feel uneasy that someone is watching you, only to turn around and find someone staring at you.

A shopping mall often leaves me exhausted, even with my psychic protection in place. The sheer amount of energy within a building, plus my own chronic health problems, can make being in public places a real challenge and often I find I must avoid crowds, but that is the reality of an empath.

Being an empath means living a life where you will randomly pick up the thoughts and experiences of others. Sometimes people misinterpret this as invading someone's space but this is not so, empaths have no control over feeling the emotions of others.

Every thought and action leaves a psychic blue print. People like me who are empathic or who are clairsentient, can sense the thoughts and feelings of others from an object or even a particular place. If you are born a natural empathy, you can learn how to somewhat control your ability and tap into it only when you want to. If you were not born overly empathic you can learn how to develop this ability that all people have to varying degrees.

Psychometry is the learned ability to retrieve information about people's personalities, thoughts, and images of their lives, from objects. A person who has developed the skill of psychometry can hold an object or touch the wall of a building and sense and read the energies that come from it. Learning psychometry is easy but it does take practice, without practicing you will never develop this gift unless you were born with it.

Select a personal item from a person you know, such as jewelry or clothing. The more contact a person has with an object, the stronger the imprint of energy. Therefore, it's easier to pick up feelings, thoughts or images. Focus on the object you are holding and relax your mind. FEEL the object, use your heart's intelligence and listen to the thoughts and feelings that come from it. Notice feelings in your body; be aware of thoughts, words and images that come to your mind. Write these down to share with the person later. Another method of clairsentience you can practice is head tapping.

Here is an example of how I would perform this, so that you can try it for yourself:

A client comes to me and her name is Debbie; she wonders what a blind date will be like for her. In my mind's eye, I stand her in front of me. I stand behind her and rest my head softly on her shoulder so that it gently touches hers. I ask her to look at the potential romantic partner she is considering. I listen to her thoughts about the person; I feel her emotions about this person. I tell her that she is going to feel that he is really a great guy, she likes his eyes and hair but she feels he might be someone who has commitment issues.

Another example of developing clairsentience is feeling a situation out for yourself or someone else. Let's say I am planning to go somewhere for a visit and I'd like to know if I will enjoy it or not. This time I'm thinking about a workshop that I am considering attending, but I am not sure about:

I focus on the name of the workshop and relaxing my mind. I feel the energy of the name of the workshop. This is very similar to holding a necklace and feeling the energy from it. The only difference is I am not holding an object but instead I am focusing on information about the object of my attention. First I will place the name in my mind's eye (I will use the name Jade's Herbal School). I focus on the name and I feel the energy that is associated with it. I might for instance get sensations of the facility being laid back and a relaxed atmosphere. To get deeper into the mood of the school, I might imagine I am walking inside the property and let my mind relax and wait for the images to come to me. I don't imagine the images or form them myself; I wait and let them appear. I see images first or I hear words or receive feelings and just allow myself to be open to any information that comes from the particular place, in this case the school.

I do this similar exercise to help others in another way:

Sometimes a client will come to me and tell me there is a certain property they are considering buying. Just as with the first exercise in which I would help someone by looking at a potential partner, I can do this same with the house. Firstly, I ask for the address and then I feel the address of the house and let my mind be relaxed and open. I hold the intention gently in my mind that I want to see this house, its flaws, and its pluses. I ask how my client will like it and what will her life be like there. I don't try to imagine a solid house; instead I allow the energy of the house to materialize to me. Often this comes as a series of close connecting energy dots, these are shadow areas, which can show up anywhere the house is damaged and needs work, but it can also show recent changes. So when I see a shadow spot or sense a shadow spot, I rest my focus on it and ask … what is this? I relax my mind and I allow my unconscious to relay information about the house to me. Next, I will stand the client in front of me and I will stand behind her looking over her shoulder. I will sense how she feels about the house, I will sense her thoughts and her reactions to the place and then I explain to her what I felt through her.

If you'd like to know what someone thinks of you, you can try this exercise:

Imagine your name written down on paper and that the person whom you are curious about is looking at it. Imagine you are standing behind her/him. How does that person feel about your name? Be aware of any thoughts, feelings and images that emerge. Just remember to always relax your mind and allow information to come to you. You cannot force it or it will not then be intuitive information.

I have another way to approach this: Let's say someone whom I shall call Debbie asks me what someone feels about her. I ask the person's name and then I imagine them standing in front of me. I feel this person's personality and then I share with Debbie some of the traits of this person that I am picking up. If I am picking up on this person's energy, then I can continue with the exercise. I then imagine that the person in question is standing in front of me and I'm standing behind them as before. I rest my head gently beside them and I sense how they feel when they look at Debbie. I am again open to sensations, thoughts, images and words that come to me.

There are many ways to use the gift of clairsentience. Use your imagination and enjoy learning the ways your intuitive mind can enhance your life. The ability of clairaudience will naturally evolve through relaxing your mind and waiting for images, thoughts and "messages" to come to you.

Each person is gifted with psychic abilities and you can learn how to strengthen those abilities in your own home and at your own pace. For most of us, developing our intuition involves us clearing our minds, grounding our energies and learning how to feel people and situations with the intelligence of our heart.

Fearful feelings and negative energies can make developing our psychic talents a challenge, and it is important to trust in your protection and do not go outside your comfort zone.

Wake Up and Feel the Vibrations

Clairvoyance seemly means "seeing clearly" it is the ability to understand grasp and interpret the information through extrasensory capabilities. The part of your brain that you access when you are developing clairvoyance is the part of your brain that is active during dreaming and visualizations. Clairvoyance doesn't mean seeing into the future, although you can see visions when peering into someone's energy field. Seeing into the future is called a seer.

Daydreaming can enhance your psychic abilities and so do this as often as you can. Sit quietly and imagine beautiful scenes in your mind's eye, such as walking along a river of sapphire blue, gazing at a waterfall and enjoy watching the water as it ripples over beautifully colored stones, creating prisms of color.

Make time for daydreaming and really try to imagine all different shades of color and how those colors "feel".

Close your eyes and imagine you are standing in a field of orange pumpkins. Their fat heads glisten happily in the sunshine, and as far as you can see, it's all just a sea of orange and green landscape. Now ask yourself how this color makes you feel. Repeat the word "orange" in your head, notice where it settles within your body. How does it affect your emotions?

When I see orange I feel strong, I feel forthright and courageous. It feels more masculine to me, more independent. Now imagine a transparent sheet of orange color and place some dirty patches within it and see how that makes you feel now that the orange is stained. For me the vibration has changed from being independent to dependent and needy, from forthright to deceiving. Do this exercise with all the colors and write them down. It's all training to get to know the vibration of color. The next step is to learn how to see color clairvoyantly around people and feel why that person is producing a certain color.

Learning to do this is easy but it does require patience and practice. First of all, get comfortable and picture a friend of a friend or friend of a relative standing in front of you. Allow your mind to relax but keep the image of the person there; there is no need to consider the details of the person's physical appearance or what they are wearing.

Ask your spirit to reveal to you (your conscious mind) the colors that surround the person you are looking at clairvoyantly. Now look at the space around the person and allow any colors to materialize. You may not see the colors though you may hear a word such as "yellow" or you just feel that the color yellow is around them. Stay in this relaxed altered mind set. The kind of relaxed feeling that you have when you are trying to go to sleep, only you aren't falling asleep, you are just being in a relaxed state. When we are relaxing our minds in this way and looking at someone, our unconscious minds can imprint information onto our conscious minds.

Practice this often with many different people and write down any information that comes to you. If you see blue around someone, let your mind rest on the blue for awhile and ask yourself "how does this blue make me feel". The tricky part when you are asking how this color makes you feel, is that you have to remember that you are attempting to pick up the emotional, physical, spiritual vibration of that color and how it relates to that person.

Perform the following exercise often:

Imagine color around a person and get a feel of how and why that color is there and how it relates to them. When you meet someone who knows the person, ask them if he or she has been feeling anxious or happy about something and see how correct you were in the information you gathered from them clairvoyantly.

The next step to this exercise is to see who or what is with them in spirit. So go through the whole process again of allowing your mind to be relaxed in that "just before you sleep" feeling.

Look at the space around the person and ask your own spirit to show you who is there with them in spirit. Allow shapes to form, don't fight it just "allow" it to happen. If you try to control it, then it is not your psychic mind at work. Do not attempt to emotionally connect with what you see; you are just observing the person's energy field. Write down who and what you see. Perhaps it will be a dog, an ancestor, angel or spiritual guide. Next shift the focus off them for an instant, and ask your spirit why this being is with them. Perhaps you'll hear an answer in your head or feel it in your heart center. Write it down and then share the information you have obtained with the person you are viewing, and see if anything relates to them.

Let's do another exercise in developing your clairvoyance. As always put up your protective shield especially over your heart area.

Get into a comfortable position and visualize someone's home that you would like to visit or perhaps a building like a church. Don't just select places where there is a lot of negativity or you could freak yourself out, and pick up unwanted entities. If you did pick up something or feel something coming at you, blue flame it right away and then surround yourself with a denser light such as gold.

Here is an example of when I performed this action so you can have a clearer idea of how to carry out this exercise.

One of my favorite places to visit is the Martyrs Shrine in midland Ontario, so this will be the place that I am visiting spirituality. It is similar to remote viewing. Once I am settled, I imagine the white light of the Great Spirit around me and I invoke my guides and angels to protect me. I imagine I am standing at the foot of the hill that leads up to the church. Just as with the other exercises, I let my mind relax, and in my mind's eye I notice a shape to the left of the church. I look at it for a little while and I notice it looks like the shape of a priest in a long robe.

Next, a movement around the church's roof catches my inner vision and I look up and I see an angel. I say *God bless you angel*. I proceed further into the grounds of the church. I am walking around the churchyard but I'm not paying attention to any details of the trees or buildings. I am placing my attention on what is lighter, spiritual and ethereal. I make sure my mind is relaxed and open to what is there spirituality. The important thing to remember is DO NOT imagine what is there, instead go there and let people, angels, animals and so forth appear to you, effortlessly and naturally. When I am leaving, I walk back to where I started from and turn to face the church and close the psychic door in front of me; this ensures I am disconnected to that place. For me the door is like a garage door that I shut and it cuts off my connection or ends my visit from the place I travelled to. Nothing can pass through my psychic door.

My friend Tom contacted me and said he felt there was a spiritual presence in his house. He asked me if I could look at his house clairvoyantly. Even though I have never been to his place, I can still have the ability to do this. It is really very simple once you get the hang of it.

Firstly, I think of Tom. I take a deep relaxing breath, feed my brain some oxygen and I let my mind relax. I think about how Tom is feeling today. Once I start feeling some of Tom's feelings I open my psychic mind a bit more. I place him in his kitchen even though I don't know what his kitchen looks like. I have been given the information that Tom lives in a house and so the energy of house/home resides in Tom's energy. So I just have to relax my mind and with the intention of wanting to see it, just allow it to happen. I think of Tom in his kitchen and let my mind relax. I ask myself how Tom feels about the "kitchen" and how do I "feel" about Tom's kitchen. Right away I "feel" or "sense" the kitchen is narrow and needs some work. I get a sense that Tom looks at his cupboards and thinks they need work done on them. I want to get a sense of if the kitchen is clean or messy today. Next, I allow my focus to expand a bit more. I want to feel what his home feels like and if it is one level or two. I also want to feel what rooms he prefers more, and what colors dominate his home. Now I let my mind be relaxed, I release a mist that will travel throughout Tom's home and this mist will reveal any spirits or entities that are in the house. I watch as the mist fills the area. I put the intention into my psychic mist that it will cling to any spirit. Through the mist I see a shape of a female. She takes form slowly. I notice how she is dressed and the feelings she gives off to me. I get a strong sense that she lived in the 1800s and she lost a child and she's been looking for this child and that is why she hasn't crossed into the light. I then fill the house with white light and ask the angels to come forward and help this lady into the light. Afterwards I inform Tom that there is woman in his house that needs help and to continue with the white light and prayers until he feels the energy in his home has lifted.

Next we will look at our clairvoyance ability to see what kind of work someone does. Think of someone you know but you don't know what they do for a living. It needs to be someone you can find out what they do for a living and how accurate you were, after you finish the exercise.

I will tune into someone to give you an example of how I do it.

Perhaps I am doing a reading and I want to get a feel for my client, so I try to find out what they do for a living. For the purpose of this exercise, let's imagine that I have Pam with me. First of all, I feel her personality, her ups and downs her likes and dislikes. I am linking with her energy with the intention of telling her things about herself. I take a deep breath in and I relax my mind. She says yes to certain things I am telling her about herself, so I know I have her energy. I think of the word "work" and imagine her standing in an empty room. I keep thinking of work in relation to her. I let my mind relax … Pam, work, Pam, work, and I let images float up to my mind. I then let words float up to my mind and I "feel" those words and those images. I will share with Pam what I am feeling and I will then pull one of my cards for her concerning work, and share with her what the card reveals. Then I link the messages and feelings around the card to Pam.

Another way to feel what a person does for a living or just enjoys doing such as a hobby, is to first focus on their hands and relax your mind and get a sense of the kinds of energies those hands intermingle with. Is it creative? Is it musical? Is it mechanical? Relax your mind and allow images, words and feelings to come to you.

Look at someone clairvoyantly to see who is around them, such as partners, family, friends and even pets.

Remember always select a person that you know you can later get information about, so you can verify what you feel or see around them. Put your protection up and then proceed with the exercise. Imagine the person you'd like to look at clairvoyantly and place them in a room with a neutral color background. Let your consciousness fan out and sense their energy field. You may notice or hear a color you may not. The intention is to see what people or pets are around them on the earth plane. This can also be done to see who is with them in spirit such as angels and ancestors.

Once you have developed your clairvoyant skills, you will be more sensitive to energies that are around you. This will allow you to avoid negative people and situations. This ability of being sensitive can be a blessing.

Chapter 7

The Green Intuitive

Being one with nature...

You and I are children of this earth, we come from this land. This sacred place gave birth to us and it bestows its knowledge unto us. When we die, we go into the spirit world and then like migrating geese in the autumn, we are drawn back to Mother Earth again and again. Mysteries whispered to our souls urge our bodies and our spirits to return to this place. Somewhere beyond the sky, I can almost see the great multitudes of spirits that rush in from other dimensions. There is a beauty to this land that connects to our spirits and it pulls us in. We enter through the gates of the four cardinal directions — east, south, west and north. I believe that is why we always turn our faces into the winds we instinctively know that the earthly breezes guide us.

So while we are here, why wouldn't we want to connect to this land? Why wouldn't we want to feel the energy of this world and respect all our relatives that live within it? People who identify themselves as a green intuitive, love Mother Earth right down to her core; they are connected to her soul, they hear her heartbeat. Our promise to our Mother is to live compassionate lives upon her. An ancient oath spoken between us and our Earth Mother was the energy that opened the gates that ushered us in ... strive to find that path to attain Earth wisdom; it is the great mystery that urges us on.

To begin the journey of becoming a green intuitive, follow the practice of connecting with plants and trees. When you're out walking, look at a plant-being and ask yourself how this plant person feels. Is their energy masculine or feminine, is the plant healthy, is it happy? Allow words, thoughts and feelings to come to you. Your aura will take on the properties of the plant and you will be able to feel what the plant feels (this is why I urge you not to connect with poisonous plants; their energy can make you feel sick). When you practice this, you are operating within a higher realm of knowing. The plant kingdom recognizes this and will usually accept the opportunity to share a part of their knowledge with you. As it is with people, it is usually the same with plants, and it is easier to introduce yourself through connecting with their gender or emotional intelligence.

This practice will pay off big time by helping you to connect quickly with the plant world.

Here is a meditation you could learn for when you are looking at herbs for perhaps a new blend of teas that you'd like to try or you are going to be using some herbal medicines.

Let us imagine you want to mix some mint and lavender together. First focus on the mint, relax your mind, neck and body and then take a breath in and breathe in the aroma of mint. Imagine the scent as green mist, the aroma of the mint filling your lungs and sinuses. Breathe in again and as you psychically inhale the energy of mint into your body, allow it to flow where it wants to. Because at the beginning of this exercise you have made a connection to mint and have felt its energy; you can track its circulation within your being. Where does it want to go? What benefit does it have on your body? Again let your mind relax and accept all the information that is given to you by the mint, your higher self and your angels, then do the same exercise with the lavender.

You have tuned into the mint and lavender separately, but next I want you to place them together in your mind's eye. Quickly reconnect with the mint. Now bring the lavender towards the mint and allow the two herbs to merge and then *feel* the connection between them. How do they feel about each other? Do they enjoy working together? Ask whatever questions come to you, but it is important that after each question is asked that you relax your mind and be open to the thoughts, words and feelings that will come to you. All it takes is practice, practice and more practice.

The thing to remember is always humble yourself to the Creator and his creation. Offer burning herbs to the Creator and Mother Earth. When you come across land that has been injured or tainted by humans, either purposefully or accidentally, it is us humans that have the ability to heal the land. So be mindful of this responsibility.

Our hearts are not only the source of our emotions but also of our intelligence. The old saying, "listen to your heart" is a very accurate statement and our intuition is never wrong. Our hearts act as a link to the mind and body. Therefore without listening to our hearts, we can never live intuitive lives. Let yourself be open and receiving of plant medicine. You do not have to drink it or inhale it to heal you. Just meditating with a plant or tree being can lift your spirits and bring peace and harmony to your heart.

A word of caution is to never eat or drink any plant without knowing if it is safe or not. Always consult with an herbalist to learn more about the plant world. I always keep to herbs that I have used many times such as lavender, mint, chamomile, rose petals and dandelion.

Select an herb that you use in healing or cooking and place the image of that herb in your mind. For the example of this meditation, I will use chamomile.

I imagine chamomile in my mind's eye and let myself relax while keeping the image of it in my mind. I look at its stem, its leaves and flowers and I let my mind relax and ask the question — *if there was a color around chamomile what would it be?* I allow an image of a color to slowly form around the plant. I watch this happen rather than make it happen. I am not placing the color around the plant; I am merely watching it form on its own. Once I see a glimpse of color I ask another question — *what does this color mean?* I ask again, what is the plant doing or thinking that is causing that color?

When you have finished this meditation, move onto the next level of this exercise. Place chamomile next to another being, such as apple, and just let your mind relax. You have been focusing a bit on chamomile, so look at that herb again just quickly enough to feel its vibration again and then look at the apple and get a feel of its energy. Sense if it is masculine or feminine or is it nice or grouchy. Then merge the two species together in your mind's eye and become aware of how the interact with each other. Do they work well together?

Always be in a relaxed state and always work with all your protection in place, because when you are doing work like this, you do open your being up, so it's always good to have that assurance of your protection.

Work from a place of serenity and peace. Be open to hearing messages from the plant people. Always continually strive to work with integrity and I'm sure you will enjoy communing with nature. It is a path well worn and we instinctively do know our way. Nature is the wisdom and beauty that binds us all together, thank her for her time and thank the plant beings for their time, let your journey begin.

Being Green is Great

I do not perform exorcisms but I do bless an area to bring in more positive energies, such as angels and fairies. There is the balancing of the elements and then working with herbs and plant energies to cleanse and protect. In my book *Walking the Path: The Cree to the Celtic*, I have recorded all my ceremonies and rituals and I have rituals to balance the elements and to bring in protection.

Blessing of Mother Earth

I often use besoms made of slim twigs from birch trees. I will use the besom to sweep the land of any negativity. Always go in a clockwise fashion and then sprinkle the land with sea salt, tobacco, corn meal or any herbs that you feel drawn to.

Connecting with Trees

Imagine yourself sitting under a large tree. The limbs of the tree curve through a canopy of green leaves. Sometimes a light breeze catches the leaves and the warmth of a late summer sun peeks out and warms your face. The breeze is light and mild. Song birds call out periodically; a cicada buzzes, and bugs and crickets hum softly in the grasses. You lift your face towards the sky and you notice that some of the leaves of the tree are soaked by sunlight and some are cloaked in shade, the tree is lush and green and it feels peaceful.

Shift your consciousness to your heart and feel this tree being. Open your heart up and feel how this tree feels, sense how healthy this plant being is. Once you have done this, say thank you to the tree being for sharing themselves with you.

Having peace of mind and being in a positive state of mind, makes for a brighter, stronger aura. We need to work on areas of our lives that are broken. Connecting to the kingdom of the plants can help us heal, their wisdom is older than we are and most are eager to help, but be beware there are those that sometimes aren't, such as belladonna. Do not venture into this realm of psychic development naïvely or vainly and assume that every plant person wants to work with you, as this is foolish. Always remember that you should ask with respect, leave an offering and then wait for the answer. If the answer is no, respect it and give thanks and move on.

Each plant and tree has their own personality. A cedar tree in my back yard may not have the same attitude as a cedar tree miles away. They are like us in the fact that each is unique and no two are alike. I met a rosemary bush once that was as ornery as an old woman and wouldn't have protected a worm. She hated where she was and wanted to be left alone. I've met other rosemary bushes that were delightful and were happy to help.

But moving back to protection, it is important to shield yourself when doing any kind of psychic work. Following is a meditation that I like to perform before I do readings or walk in the woods to talk to plants and trees.

We can become enlightened through contact with the plant people and it is possible to join with other intelligent beings of various species and learn from them. We burn plants for cleansing, we drink herbs to bring healing, we burn their wood to bring warmth and visions, and we carry them as protection from evil. Give yourself a beautiful present and try standing under a tree. Be aware of the dappled sunlight around you and soak up the beauty from the tree and give thanks for its shade. Now take a moment and just be in the presence of this being and listen to the tree's spirit. That tree has kept the memories of everything that has happened since its birth. But there is more that the tree knows; it can feel your emotions and your troubles. The Earth designed us to be linked and dependent on each other. In her wisdom, she knew that life needed to be connected ... Mother Earth's web.

Our Earth Mother can satisfy our deepest hunger, her beauty brings relief from our burdens, her forests are dark and decadent and they awaken within us a desire to explore and go on sacred journeys.

In learning the ritual of smudging, it is important to be in a state of being that is receptive to becoming relaxed and peaceful, so select a time when you can be in that state of mind. Close your eyes and take a couple of deep breaths, wiggle your toes and be in the moment. You are coming to Mother Earth and the kingdom of the healers (plants) to be cleansed, so be in a subdued and appreciative state.

Chapter 8

The Aura

The colors of our souls...

The aura is layers of light that surround the bodies of all living things: it is a light that emanates from the spirit of people, animals and plants. Anything alive has a spirit and therefore has an aura.

Your aura is the glow that emanates from your eternal flame, a radiating light that is part of the cosmos. The colors of our auras are the shades of our consciousness. We are jewels of color, painted by the Creator. What are the shades of our love and sadness? When we gaze with longing at Grandmother Moon, do we glisten in translucent shades of silver and blue? We are a symphony of color that covers Mother Earth. Our colors are our spiritual fingerprint, no two are exactly alike.

Every shade of aura has a specific meaning that is unique to each of us. Working as an intuitive, you will develop ways of tapping into the aura, and the colors you see and feel will tell you a story about that person's life.

Spontaneously throughout my life, I have seen full auras. Although this was just at random times, it did give me the opportunity to see how beautiful our spiritual bodies are. I usually see auras clairvoyantly and I would like to share with you how I started doing this.

To begin learning this ability, select someone you know and in your mind's eye imagine they are standing across from you in a room. Now with your mind in a relaxed state, gaze at the space that surrounds their body. Like a feather softly caressing your cheek, bring the thought that there is color there softly across your conscious mind. Keeping your mind relaxed, gaze at the space and allow any glimpses of color, feeling of color, or word of color, to bubble up into your conscious mind.

When I allow my mind to relax, I switch over to an altered state of consciousness. Information from my unconscious can then surface up to my conscious mind and give me information. It is the same state that you are in when you are about to fall asleep; although we don't actually fall asleep we just want to achieve a state of relaxation and openness. After doing readings for a while you will notice as soon as you look at something and let your mind relax, it is a cue to your unconscious mind to start to allow information to flow into your conscious mind and therefore you will become quicker at receiving that information.

You will soon discover whether you like doing this exercise with your eyes open or shut, many people prefer to have their eyes closed but I prefer to have my own open.

You could find someone to stand in front of you so you can practice seeing their aura, but usually you will be just visualizing someone in your mind's eye.

Select a subject, and in your imagination, place them in front of you at a distance of a yard or less. Visualize the person standing in front of a neutral shade of color, such as beige or grey. Don't worry about details of their facial features or what they are wearing as the purpose here is to discover the colors surrounding them. Be aware of the whole of them. What I mean by this is seeing them clairvoyantly and feeling them empathically; allow your focus to include the body plus the space around them.

From now on when you are doing psychic work, the person will not be just their physical body but the *whole* spiritual body, which is the aura. When you are viewing someone or something, there will be an area or areas that will quickly draw your attention. The area may just look like a dark bubble or patch. If you are drawn to any area that is darkened or bright, just look at that spot for a while. Let your mind rest on it, and ask yourself what it means, and how it is affecting this person. Let your mind be relaxed and open to hearing messages from *your* spirit.

Depending on what shade of intelligence you are viewing, you might hear a word like "anger" or "angel" or you might get a certain feeling, let it come to you and then let it go.

Looking at the person and the energy surrounding the body, take notice of any sensations of color, size and shape. You can jot things down on a pad if you like. A person with a larger aura is generally healthy, spiritual, outgoing and loves people. A person with a smaller aura would be introverted, shy, have potential health problems or are just lacking in sleep or proper nutrition.

When you are looking at someone's energy field, make sure your protection is in place. If you sense any draining of your energy, reinforce your protection and withdraw from connecting. You could be making a connection with a negative person or a negative entity. If you feel ungrounded, have anxiety or any feeling that is unpleasant, take a moment to *blue flame* yourself before you continue.

In my work as a psychic healer, I have sometimes seen entities attached to people. They often appear to me as black shapes with an arm like attachment to a person's body, most often in the crown chakra. The following list is a guide to what these entities may mean.

Entities in the crown chakra	Confusion, out of touch with reality, depression, suicidal thoughts, feeling the divine has abandoned you, anger.
Entities in the brow chakra	Racing thoughts, obsessive thoughts, hallucinations, migraines, mental illness.
Entities in the throat chakra	Difficult to communicate, throat disorders, thyroid problems, fear, being argumentative, feeling like you have no free will.

Entities in the heart chakra	Heart problems, heartless, anger, feelings of being worthless, paranoid.
Entities in the solar plexus	Control issues, aggression, hatred.
Entities in the sacral chakra	Extreme emotions, self-absorbed, sexual problems, illness, living in fear, addictions.
Entities in the root chakra	Sexual addictions, sexual impotency, self-absorbed, controlling.

Sometimes when I view this negative energy, I will hear a word associated with it like "Ouija board" and I'll ask them if they use a spirit board and if they do or have done, I advise them not to use this type of device as it attracts entities on lower realms.

Explain to clients that these attachments can cause depression and anxiety, in fact all kinds of mental problems, but they can get rid themselves of it. What I suggest to people is to smudge daily and perform the smudging ritual along with prayer until they feel it has lifted, also ask for the angels remove all negative entities from their aura.

I always pray for a person after a reading and especially for people with energy attachments that are dark.

You may see people whose auras appear to be shattered or fractured. It is my thought that these people have endured many hardships and trauma. If you see this, just focus on one of the lines in the fractures, let your mind relax and ask *your* spirit what happened, what does this fracture mean? Relay that information to your client, but if you come across something that is from the past and very sensitive, you can choose not to share it or you can cushion what you feel. You should never lie to a client but you can chose not to share something, especially if it is something painful from their past.

When I see angels, guides and totem spirits, I usually see them first as a ball of light. I will let my focus rest on that light for a while and ask what it is, and then I wait for the being of light to reveal itself to me. The distance between an angel, guide, ancestor or fairy is relevant to how spiritual and or how interactive that person is with that energy being.

For example, imagine I see an angel, but the angel looks faraway, this suggests to me that an angel is willing to work with the person but the person themselves hasn't reached out for the help yet. I will ask an angel to flash me the color of the chakra that I need to focus on in my reading. If an angel flashes me red for instance, then I know there are issues around the root chakra. I will look away from the client and I will ask to see the person's root chakra in my mind's eye. I want to feel the issues in my heart area of what is going on in the root chakra. Words may come to me such as "lack of control" or "self-loathing" or images about the person's life may surface. I usually take a moment and write things down that I pick up and then go over it in a very kind and compassionate manner. You are dealing with people's lives and you must walk in love. If you don't, the angels and other beings of light will not be willing to work with you.

If you are looking at an aura clairvoyantly and you notice a sharp line of where one color ends and another begins, take note of the color. Let's say that color is purple, and it suddenly turns to yellow. To me that that says the person was working on issues around one chakra and then working on issues linked to another chakra. You can go deeper and focus on the line where one color ends and the other starts and ask "when". If for instance you hear the word November, you can ask your client if they had some changes in their life around that time. Look at the line of where one color ends and another begins and ask "why". If you were to hear the word "separation" ask your client if this word means anything to them.

I always notice the shade of color around a person's head and this tells me what kind of thoughts and mental health this person has.

Purple around a head tells me that this person is spiritual and perhaps working on intuition instead of judgment. If the color is dirty, it could be migraines or other illness related to the head area.

Also notice how the energy flows. If it is feathery and nice looking that means the persons thoughts are flowing evenly and are relatively positive. If the energy is low and chaotic, this could mean anger, confusion and depression.

I will perceive the energy in one way and you will perceive it another, so the best advice I can give you is to write things down as you see them and this will be your reference — your teaching manual. You'll notice trends and patterns of how you see and feel things. When looking at energy, always ask your inner knowing questions ... remain quiet and you will receive the answers.

When I look at someone and they are facing me, the future is always on the right side of them (which is actually their left side). What I see to the left of them is their past. If I see images in a person's aura on the right side, then it relates to an event, which is still to come. In addition, if I see a color to the right side of them, then it is a healing color for them or perhaps issues related to the particular chakra that resonates with that color.

A practice of mine that I would hope work for others is grounding and clearing by linking with the healing beings of the plant world. For example, if I am doing psychic work and I begin to feel drained, I imagine something like a strawberry. I will think about this fruit the smell of it, the color of it and the taste of it. I focus on the nutrients of this berry and then I shower myself in its vibration.

Another example is that often when I am doing readings, I can begin to feel depleted and kind of toxic, especially if the people I have been linking with have had a lot of issues. In this case, I will imagine a plant such as asparagus. I take a few moments and I mediate quickly on the texture, the smell, color and taste of this vegetable. I imagine swallowing it and allow the plant to show me how it heals the body and then I just allow the vitality of that plant to cleanse my body and aura.

I hope that you will give some of these processes of clearing and grounding a try and experience for yourself the embodiment of healing that is available to us from the earth.

Layers of the Aura and the Chakras

From my research and my experience tuning into the human aura, I see that the aura is composed of seven layers that are powered by the chakra system. The physical body, the aura and the chakras, are one working energy body, each intertwined with each other. If any of these bodies of energy become damaged, it would cause illness or death. When I am tuning into a person and I ask to see the level of energy that deals with health, then I see something that appears like curtains falling away (so that one curtain is left standing), and then I look at that shimmering light clairvoyantly and see how healthy it is.

Looking at the energy within the human aura:

The first layer is the etheric body and it is the closest layer to the physical body. A grayish white, it is related to the root chakra and it connects the body to the higher realms.

The second layer is the emotional body and is associated with feelings; the colors change in this layer depending upon the feelings being experienced. This layer usually extends about three to five inches from the body.

The third layer of the aura is associated with our mental thoughts. This layer also holds our mental processes, it sometimes has a yellowish glow that can be seen around the head and shoulders but the hue can be affected by the person's thoughts. This layer can extend five to eight inches around the body.

The fourth layer is an important link to the spiritual plane. When we are developing our intuition we must learn to feel and listen to our heart's wisdom. This layer in our aura is the bridge between the lower vibrations of the physical world and the higher vibrations of the spiritual world.

The fifth layer or etheric template is a blue print of the physical body, which is in existence before the physical body is formed. This layer can be deeply affected by healing energies; healers will see this auric vibration extending one and half to two feet from the body.

The sixth layer or celestial layer of the aura is the spiritual emotional plane and it extends two to three feet from the body. Through this level, we experience bliss and spiritual joy. The colors of this layer have an opalescent quality.

The seventh layer of the aura extends about three to three and a half feet from the body, and it is also named the Ketheric Template. This layer is associated with the crown chakra and contains our life plans and our sacred contracts with other beings.

The Chakra System

The word "chakra" is a Sanskrit word, meaning "wheel". The chakras begin at the base of the spine and move up through the head. Many healers describe them as wheels of rotating energy. Each chakra vibrates at a different speed; the size and brightness of the wheels vary depending upon a person's spiritual enlightenment. Each chakra produces its own color and can be stimulated by their colors, which are red, orange, yellow, green, blue, indigo and violet.

Red: past life issues, courage, being grounded, independent, tribal issues, money and survival capabilities.

Orange: fertility, creativity, sexual issues, money, fidelity and feelings of self worth.

Yellow: personal power, fulfillment, knowledge, self-control and mental clarity.

Green: relationships, trust, love, guilt, forgiveness and peace.

Blue: communications, speech, free will, organization and emotions, convictions and beliefs.

Indigo: intuition, psychic abilities, perceptions, memory and fears.

Violet: wisdom, inspiration, awareness, meditation and visionary.

Aura Color Meanings

Yellow

Bright Yellow	Optimistic, helpful, social and friendly.
Golden Yellow	Divine protection and wisdom.
Muddy Yellow	Fearful, depression, anti social and anger.

Red

Red	Physical, active, sexual energy, aggression and action.
Muddy Red	Anger, violence, meanness and aggression.

Orange

| Orange | Physical, independent, enjoys people but treasures alone time, bores easily and loves excitement. |
| Muddy Orange | Loner, sexual dysfunction, manipulative and anger. |

Green

| Green | Analytical, healing, tolerant but needs peace and loves the outdoors usually has a green thumb. |
| Muddy Green | Confusion, fearful and perhaps illness. |

Blue

| Blue | Loving, giving, trustworthy and spiritual. |
| Muddy Blue | Unforgiving, resentment, distrustful and spiritually unbalanced. |

Purple

| Purple | Old soul, spirituality secure, open to higher vibrations, intuitive and a healer. |
| Muddy Purple | Fearful, controlling, selfish, deceitful and closed minded |

Pink flashes in an aura, indicates love.

Silver flashes in an aura is protection, intuitive thoughts, creative thoughts and can be angels and guides.

Gold flashes in an aura is protection, wisdom and strength and also be guardians such as guides and angels.

Grey blotches in aura can be depression, illness and mental confusion, dark side of the personality, and entities.

Black blotches in an aura can be trauma from past lives, anger, hatred, sickness, sadness, entities, deceit and a dangerous person.

Brown blotches in an aura, if clear, show a love of the outdoors. If this is muddy, it can mean sickness or depression.

White is protection and purity, but it can also be guides, angels and ancestral spirits.

Muddy white can be sickness and addictions.

Mustard blotches can be pain, illness, lack of interest and apathy. (If I come across a person who has lots of mustard in their aura they are almost impossible for me to read, and I do believe it is because they have no intense pleasure in anything in their lives. They don't really love or really hate, basically they are emotionless.)

Your aura is a masterpiece created by the source of all creation The Great Mystery; your Earth Mother gave you your breath of life, she watches you grow and keeps you alive.

Each of us has a journey; the flame inside of you is your guiding light.

Chapter 9

Playing Card Meanings (Cartomancy)

Divination can be part of a spiritual path or it can stand alone, divination can show the possible outcomes of certain situations, it can also show us ways to heal by revealing what is really going on in our unconscious minds.

What does the future hold for me? Will I be successful? Does she love me? Throughout the ages and across many cultures people have asked similar questions and some have turned to the ancient art of divination for answers. Often times we find ourselves at a crossroads in our life and sometimes it seems like there is a multitude of directions we can take, each path is clouded in the unknown. Choices can seem confusing even frightening, we seek our answers in the cards; we trust the guidance of our souls and with each new direction given it is an opportunity for growth and inspiration.

As I have mentioned earlier, divination is my form of healing and working with others to heal. The cards give me clues to what is going on in a person's life, and when I'm doing a reading for myself, they show feelings, attitudes and beliefs inside of me. Looking at the cards is like looking at a photograph of your soul. When you get to know your cards, you know it is the truth staring you in the face. There are issues that must be dealt with, and the beauty of divination and working with our intuitive abilities is that there will be suggestions in the cards and we can know the way.

We are all born with an Inner Guidance system

Naturally when someone has developed their skills, usually the next step is doing readings for others. No matter how long you do readings and how confident you are in your psychic abilities, you will meet people who are extremely difficult to tune into. Sometimes it is anxiety or skepticism, which cause this, and although a person may think they are open, they may be blocking the reading subconsciously. If a person is a rather private person, then there is the vibration of "keep out" and this is a block as well. It might be the environment that is causing the blockage: the people, building and surrounding area, can all have an impact on a reader. If we cannot feel their desires and fears, then we cannot forge a psychic connection with them. It is in those cases that having knowledge of a divination tool comes in handy, such as the cards.

In this chapter on divination, we'll look at the meanings of the cards and how they relate to each other and how to match up the meaning of the cards with the energy of the sitter.

The cards are a tool that a psychic will use to guide them towards areas of interest in a clients life. Just like a torch guides you in the dark, so does a deck of cards guide you around a person's life. As I had pointed out earlier, according to ancient beliefs there are four aspects of our nature that we must balance, our minds, bodies, spirits and emotions. This is why I enjoy using playing cards, because each suit represents each aspect of the human psyche.

Hearts are concerned with love, family and home matters, and the element here is fire.
Spades are power, transformations, challenges and wisdom, so the energy is water.
Clubs are about work, education and our creative processes, so this suit is earth.
Diamonds relate to money, values and concerns around our earthly existence, so this suit is intellectual and it is air.

When doing a reading you will have several cards laid out before you. The first thing you should notice are the suits and the element that goes with each one. The element that is associated with the suit either enhances or blocks the flow of energy from a card. The elements of the suits can also weaken the energy of cards within a spread.

Using playing cards for divination goes back hundreds of years. There are 52 cards in a deck, four suits and one or two jokers. There are two colors — the red and the black, and 12 faces of nobility. No matter where you live in this world, people are familiar with playing cards. Compare it to our year: there are 52 weeks in a year, 4 seasons, and the 12 crown cards equal the 12 months of the year.

Ace is new beginnings, it is the hope of what we desire, the start of a cycle.

Two seeks union and co-operation. This card is about partnerships, but two can fear being alone.

Three shows us new opportunities, decisions that need to be made, and communications between people. Threes can be confused and uncertain, but are also carefree.

Four is stable, dependable, and serious. It is a card that represents service and duty. The feelings towards home is felt here and matters around family.

Five is energy and a craving for new experiences; it shows restlessness in a person, adventure, unafraid to try something new, moving, and being versatile about people and situations.

Six is about balance, debts being paid and karma being fulfilled. The restless energy of five has given way to the desire for rest and recuperation. The vibration of six doesn't want to move forward, it wants to stop and rest. But debts and favors that are owed must be dealt with.

Seven is about reflections, looking at the inner self, worry and stress. Under the vibration of this card we are analyzing, researching trying to figure out how to move through obstacles.

Eight is about control and power. The energy of this card is social, talking to people about work, love, parties, and business meetings. Eights are successful and bold and there is wealth around this number.

Nine is about letting go and if we resist it could be removed from our lives. The vibration of this number is transformation, renewal after a period of struggle, new cycles and new relationships.

Ten is the number of fulfillment and achievements. The vibration of this number is success but can be obsessive. Rest and be happy for a while, you are in a new cycle anything is possible. Keep the wisdom you've learned from the lesser numbers.

Jacks as people are younger people, or people who are young at heart. As situations, they can represent people coming in and out of our lives at a fast pace, events being short lived, and communications between people such as letters, emails and phone calls.

Queens as people are women, or men who are feminine. These are people of some authority in your lives and it can even represent the client, it is also a card of wisdom. As a situation, the vibration of this card is concerned with home and family but it can also bring restrictions and burdens.

Kings as people are male and can be a masculine female. These are people who have authority and power and can represent the client in a reading. The energy of this card is power and visionary. Under the vibration of a king, there can be a saving grace and power to avert disaster.

Cartomancy: Learning the Meanings of the Cards

Spades

Ace of Spades (Complete Change). Traditionally, this card represents death or an ending, but it is also about new beginnings and powerful transitions happening in a person's life, which can be negative or positive, depending on surrounding cards. This is an ace card so it shows the desires of the person: I WANT, I DESIRE. Another warning with this card is an issue could be using up most of your time and energy due to speculation and worry. This is a power card; it represents the force of upheaval and change, either for the positive or negative, but either way, when events happen they will be traumatic.

Two of Spades (Deceit). This card is about relationships and our fears about being alone. Under the influence of this card, there is a need for agreement, but some issues need to be dealt with before peace can happen, so make sure you are dealing with an honest person. The energy behind this card is a lying friend or partner.

Three of Spades (Apprehension). This card is about being worried and stressed about people and events that are going on. There could be a break of a relationship due to the meddling of a negative person. Worrying never solves any problems, it just makes us ill. You could receive troubling news, be careful with your health during this time and be kind to yourself.

Four of Spades (Recuperation). This card is about resting after a stressful time. There is the possibility of having to make decisions rather quickly. Things will now continue to recover slowly. If you have been ill or depressed, things will ease by spring. Take time to take extra care of yourself.

Five of Spades (Departures). This card is about farewells and separations. It is time to cut your ties and move on. This could mean leaving a job, a place of dwelling or a person. The energy of this card is about breaking free and unexpected surprises.

Six of Spades (Seer). You need to be aware of what is holding you prisoner, what is keeping you stuck? There are events and people who are destined to test you to see if you are brave enough to advance. Can you stand outside your movie and observe what is going on? Try to see things from another's point of view.

Seven of Spades (Eliminate). To avoid possible danger it is wise to withdraw from negative people, people you know who insult you, criticize you constantly, try to push you around and just use you. There may be disruption among friends. It is time for you to spend some quality time with yourself and find your inner happiness.

Eight of Spades (Worrier). Conflicts with family, and/or issues with friends, can be resolved through compromise. The energy of this card centers on work and health, or money and health. Increased concerns around financial matters, and pressures from people, will lead to arguments and quarrels. You are at a cross-roads and you must make positive changes.

Nine of Spades (Determination). There will be obstacles for you to deal with; these are lessons in your journey. Failure may precede success and that is okay, we learn from our mistakes.

Under the influence of this card you may have to double your efforts, so if you are looking for a job, you may have to try extra hard. Watch your health if you feel unwell get to a doctor as soon as possible.

Ten of Spades (Fear). If we couldn't feel fear, we wouldn't be able to protect ourselves and loved ones. Pressures of home and business could cause delays and interference. Worrisome news about a friend or business associate looms and you could be forced to end a friendship or partnership. You have let things go so far that now it is impossible to fix and you must move in a new direction. No turning back.

Jack of Spades (Duality). The positive side to this card is that the person loves to work hard for something they believe in, and the influence of this energy, is tremendous sacrifice in order to achieve success. The negative side is a person who is jealous, stuck but can be charming and deceiving, you need to be on your toes when dealing with this individual.

Queen of Spades (Betrayer). As a person, this card is a female whom you cannot trust. She interferes with others; she loves money, is completely self-absorbed and is difficult to please. As a situation, this card means that you need to be aware of a person, male or female, or dealings with people who are calculating and crave power.

King of Spades (Authority). As a person, this is a man who is over someone or has authority over you. Look at the surrounding cards to see if they are negative or positive as it will provide a clue to what energy he is in your life, either good or bad. As a situation, it can mean legal matters and something that will surprise you, which could be unsettling as spades brings change and sometimes the changes aren't what we desire.

Clubs

Ace of Clubs (Success). Most, if not all, your endeavors will be successful. This card means that fate, luck, and divine help, are on your side to help you succeed. The energy around this card coming up in a reading also means financial gains, new job or promotion around work. It also means lots of communicating with people in general and success around education. There could be good news coming and new beginnings. This card shows the desire of the client in a reading, remember it is an ace card and it means I WANT.

Two of Clubs (News). You could be pulled in many directions, so try to stay focused. If surrounding cards are positive, then dealings with other people are favorable, if not then beware as business dealings or friendships could become strained. Care is needed around this card in dealings with others. You will hear news from someone you know concerning work, school or business.

Three of Clubs (Creativity). The energy of this card is creative, restless and prone to indecisions. You would like a change in your life and to be more social. Under the influence of this card, there will be more outings and friendly gatherings. People who are like-minded or who are in similar work will be coming your way, and some doors that were previously closed to you, may soon be opened. New ideas, new avenues for creative expressions, happiness in the arts, and important communications in work are indicated.

Four of Clubs (Work). The energy of this card is stability and focus, in other words you know what you want and you have a pretty good idea how to get it. It also means working and work related things will be important to you, such as taking care of your home, buying items for your home, a car etc. You are in a stable position in life where others can depend on you. You're happy where you are at, in terms such as work, school and creative progress.

Five of Clubs (Cleanse). You are not happy where you are at, you would like to change directions. You would like to refresh your whole life and that includes people, environment and your lifestyle. Definitely some areas of your life need revamping and under the influence of clubs, you will begin to get serious about doing this. Enjoy the physical energy of this card, you will be free spirited and opened minded, change will be like a breath of fresh air.

Six of Clubs (Movement) is a card about travel and transitions but being anchored, so lots of moving but not necessary moving from one place to another although that is not out of the question. If you are moving then the move will go smoothly. Travel plans will be stable and fun. This card is also about improvements around home and family or close friendships.

Seven of Clubs (Trapped). This card signifies some deep thinking going on, analyzing and evaluating the odds or the outcome of a situation or person. Feelings of being trapped can be associated with this card. Avoid any get rich schemes or partnering with people whom you don't know well. Beware of empty promises and squabbles among friends.

Eight of Clubs (Take a Break). The love of money, work, and activity might become all consuming. When this card appears in a reading, it is time to step back and take a breather as you're getting ahead of yourself. There is power in this card, there is an energy that is either in your life or about to come into your life that will help you attain your goals, but your wellbeing must be guarded and taken care of for things to go smoothly.

Nine of Clubs (Energetic). There is the energy of success with this card, the drive to get things finished, wrap things up and to keep promises to others. Whatever projects you are working on, or relationships you have been thinking about ending or starting, will be happening now or within a few weeks of this card appearing in a reading.

Ten of Clubs (Completion). The vibration of this card is the completing of projects, the highest you can go in a certain field of work. You have become an expert at career — an accumulation of knowledge around an experience that taught you many things about work, school and health. Reaching a certain plateau, perhaps you have worked hard to lose 20 pounds and your part way there, this card is all about reaching a milestone.

Jack of Clubs (Changes) as a person it usually represents a younger person but can identify with people who are young at heart. As a situation, the energy of this card is eccentric, unconventional and you can expect the unexpected. A youthful card.

Queen of Clubs (Authority). This card is about having to answer to someone who is either female or has feminine traits such as being sensitive to others feelings. The energy is wisdom, beauty and a need for perfection.

King of Clubs (Power). When this card is representing a man, it can mean someone significant in your life or it can mean a masculine woman. If it is representing a situation, then it means power, confidence but a sense of burden and restrictions.

Diamonds

Ace of Diamonds (Prosperous). This card can mean messages or news of a financial nature, and the news will be about a significant gain in finances. This is an ace card so it represents your desire, the I WANT in the reading. Look to the cards beside it to figure out the meaning. Will it be good news about money, work, and creative endeavors or not?

Two of Diamonds (Advantageous Contacts). This card's message is about unions and working with someone to attain a goal. There will be invitations to events and happy gatherings; there could even be discussions around subjects about money, contracts and business, and it can also mean a financial windfall.

Three of Diamonds (Confusion). The energy around this card appearing in a reading is confusion around money and things we are responsible for, such as people, pets and jobs. There is restless energy and perhaps loss of money or job. Legal problems surround this card. Remember under the three vibration there are always opportunities, forks in the road, so choose wisely.

Four of Diamonds (Harmony). Now the energy of this card brings a desire to be more stable and to make sure that job, home and all financial concerns are being taken care of. Under the four vibration there will be a stronger foundation and the peace of mind, which that kind of security brings.

Five of Diamonds (Transitions). This card suggests changes in financial situations; this could be a time of changing jobs or investments. Changing attitudes around money and work can occur under the vibration of this card.

Six of Diamonds (Balance). This card is about paying off debts, making sure there is money for all your needs and being concerned about duty to others. Money owed to you could come in, depending on the surrounding cards in a reading. Resting and taking it easy is important right now before moving onto another phase in life.

Seven of Diamonds (Thrifty). This is a card that foretells of financial problems. Be careful to not overspend at this time, avoid shopping sprees and unnecessary extras. This is not a good time for investments or making loans.

Eight of Diamonds (Windfall). This card is about receiving unexpected money, such as loans being repaid, bonus at work and money owned to you from government. Monetary gains will be coming your way. The power of eight brings us back to where we feel we are on steady ground.

Nine of Diamonds (Parting). The vibration of nine is letting go, so you can expect some of your cash leaving your wallet. Hang onto your savings and be careful where you spend your cash and what on. Expect unexpected bills to arise.

Ten of Diamonds (Abundance). This card foretells a time of plenty and abundance. Fortune will arrive due to hard work and commitment to a goal, job or education. Positive changes are coming, great time for investments or starting a business.

Jack of Diamonds (Communications). News is coming to you possibly from a young man or someone young at heart. There can be confusion or anxiety with this card, for you or someone close to you, concerning money.

Queen of Diamonds (Indulgence). As a situation, this card is about treating yourself. You will be spending some of your cash on something that you and your loved ones enjoy. As a person, this female is coming into your life or is in your life and she loves excitement, but she can be a gossip so beware of what you say.

King of Diamonds (Provider). As a situation it means that finances will be okay, you will be able to provide for your family now and in the near future. As a person, it represents a male person who is a good business man and will be involved in your financial affairs.

Hearts

Ace of Hearts (Bliss). Being an ace card this shows our desires, I WANT. This card has an emphasis on relationships and nurturing and depicts our desire for love. This is a home card, a relationship card, there could be good news coming from a loved one or friend. An ending of a dispute.

Two of Hearts (Companionship). This is a card of unions and relationships, a need to be with someone or hang out with friends. Under this vibration, there is a need to be with other people.

Three of Hearts (Chaos). This card may show indecision and confusion around a relationship, and there could be more than one love interest. Three is a restless number, so it can indicate a lack of commitment. Be cautious when this card appears.

Four of Hearts (Peace). This card is about peace and stability. It is a blessing to have harmony in our lives. This card shows this energy is either with you now or coming in soon. The energy of the four of hearts, augers a stable and happy phase, and if single and in a love relationship, it could be a marriage proposal or taking a relationship to a deeper level.

Five of Hearts (Turmoil). This card means changes around home, family and friends, so beware of quarrels. Partings could be divorce or separation, or it could be someone in the family is leaving home for school. Consequently, this card can mean either, so look to surrounding cards for clues.

Six of Hearts (Increased Clarity). This card means that there will be healing after hurting. People coming together to talk things through, clearing all negativity that has been eating up joy. Conversations about commitment and helping one another may come to light and clear up many misunderstandings.

Seven of Hearts (Disappointments). The energy of this card is of being disappointed by a friend or a loved one. Broken promises, lack of commitment, confusion and a sense of depression around matters of the heart. Inner reflection is needed and beware of becoming a martyr for others.

Eight of Hearts (Passionate Encounters). This card is about attending parties, gatherings going out to restaurants etc. Being more social than usual and meeting interesting people, perhaps an invitation to a wedding or baptism. There is the possibility that you could meet someone, a love interest, in the coming months.

Nine of Hearts (Endings). This is traditionally the wish card and so it is very lucky to have this appear in a spread, but it is also a nine, so there are endings associated with it. In endings, there are beginnings, new horizons to explore, fresh starts.

Ten of Hearts (Good News). This card is about beginnings and accomplishments, and when you are under the vibration of this card, it could mean a couple of things. First, it can mean that a relationship is going to go to a much deeper level, such as marriage or that you have decided to start a family. However, it can also mean that a family or friendship has come through a difficult time and has attained peace and stability.

Jack of Hearts (Friend). This card usually represents a friend in the reading, look at surrounding cards to get an idea of the state of the friendship.

Queen of Hearts (Love). This card can represent a woman in the client's life, so look to surrounding cards to give you a clue of her character and her reason to appear in the reading. As a situation it can mean engagement or marriage.

King of Hearts (Kind Hearted). This card can represent a loving male in your life, in the past, present or future. Look at surrounding cards to get an idea of what his purpose is. As a situation, it can mean the birth of a child, adoption or new pet.

Mini Celtic Cross

This spread has six cards. You place one card down on a level surface in a vertical position and then one on top horizontally (cards 1 and 2). Place the rest in a line to the right of the crossing cards, starting with the bottom card (cards 3–6). The position meanings are below.

1st card – The heart of the matter.
Main issue, major concern, problem.

2nd card – That which is crossing you.
Source of resistance, what opposes the problem, influences.

3rd card – That which is beneath you.
The source of your problem, the root cause of an issue.

4th card – Past.
Something from the past that is still influencing the present could be a person, trait, fear or concern and so on.

5th card – What's on your mind.
Assumptions, convictions, beliefs, desired result you'd like to see happen.

6th card – Future.
Person, event, belief, what must be considered, what is coming.

It is so important to understand the meaning of your card positions, so you don't have to think about them anymore and when giving a reading, you can relax and allow your unconscious mind to send to your conscious mind, visions, pictures, feelings and words.

Notice the elements, which ones are missing, which ones are enhancing or opposing each other and which elements are in excess.

In the Celtic spread look at several cards together such as 1 and 2 (see below), read their meanings separately and then notice the elements.

Let us say you have a Queen of Clubs in the first position (first card laid), and in the second position (card crossing it) you have a King of Hearts. First, read the meaning of each card. Notice the elements right away. You'll see that the king is a heart and the queen is a club. Earth and fire are friendly, so this couple is harmonious, or if reading the cards as a situation, it means harmony. Since the card in position 3 is the root of the problem and position 5 card is about your attitude and beliefs, see if the elements balance themselves out in those positions or not. For example if you have in position 3 the two of clubs and in position 5 the nine of diamonds, you could say that the clubs being earth, weaken the air in the diamonds, and this could mean that the desire to start new projects or possibly moving could be hampered by losing money.

Look at the cards in the positions of past and future to see if the elements are compatible, and if so then the flow is going easy in a person's life. If not, it will be a bumpy road. In cards where you have a negative message, for example the ten of spades (where health could be an issue due to stress), but the outcome is a two of diamonds (which is a positive card and the elements are positive with each other), then I know I may go through a difficult time, but it will be softened by the blessings from the two of diamonds.

Chapter 10

Creating and Working with Your Own Oracle Deck

Handmade oracle decks are very effective because you are imbuing each card with the beauty of your vibration. In this chapter, I will explain to you how to make more sets of your own oracle cards and how to use them.

Oracle decks are a set of cards used for divination. They are not divided up into suits like in cartomancy or tarot; usually oracle decks don't have any divisions at all. Most if not all oracle cards have a theme such as angels or nature. The cards are a tool to reveal what is hidden thus helping you find to that inspiration and insight to move forward in your life.

In this chapter, I will show you how to create your own oracle deck. All that is left for you to do is buy the materials to make the cards.

Dragonfly Medicine Cards

The Seven Directions Reading involves you taking your deck of "playing cards", and you or the subject selects one or two cards for each of the seven directions (meanings below). This is the first step in the reading. Then you or the subject selects a card from your own homemade oracle deck, which I call Dragonfly Medicine Cards (see below how to make them).

Dragonfly Medicine

I use Dragonfly Medicine because this energy is associated with healing with color. This medicine connects us with the power of color as colors have an amazing ability to transform our lives. Color recharges us, replenishes and harmonizes us. Dragonfly Medicine teaches us how through color, we can attract what we desire in life.

These cards will reveal your healing color. Colors affect our emotions and our senses. Colors can energize us, they can calm us and they can bring us into a state of being where healing can take place. Using color to restore balance and peace to our lives is relatively easy, such as drinking water that you have energized with color. You do this by visualizing a certain color permeating the water. Alternatively, you can meditate with a certain color by imagining yourself breathing it into your body. You can also buy a scarf or material of a healing color, and wear it or place it where you can see it throughout the day.

The Card Colors

The colors of the cards are the colors of the human chakra system except for the white card, which I included because white is universally a healing shade.

We are a rainbow of color. Our colors are the language of our spirit and our emotions. Each color has its own unique vibration, and meditating on a color can have an influence on our health and wellbeing.

For example, meditating on blue can have a calming effect on the brain, blue can leave us feeling cool and refreshed. Yellow is the morning sun warm on our faces, it is butterflies dancing around a mustard field on a summer's day. Yellow lifts us out of our doldrums and carries us to happier places.

Making a few changes to our daily lifestyle by adding color to our diet, our surroundings and our spiritual life can move us away from negative habits and behavior.

Working with the Dragonfly Oracle Deck can help you realize that you are color, you are constantly changing and you are unique.

The power animal dragonfly, links us to the healing power of color to manifest what we desire in life. This powerful totem also helps us to peel away beliefs and opinions we have about ourselves. This earthly teacher can help us re-connect with our own nature and it is when we connect with our own spirit we have the ability to choose wisely.

*Note: You can have more colors than what is listed here. I use the colors of the chakras because those colors are the most prevalent.

Materials Needed:

Decorating the cards is fun. Consider a trip to your local arts and craft store for inspiration.

Cards can be cut out of card stock to the desired size and what feels comfortable in your hands. Alternatively, use an art pad, of which the paper is denser than writing paper. Cards should be approximately the same size as the playing cards or a bit larger. You will need extra paper in seven colors; yellow, red, blue, indigo, orange, green, violet, plus white. This can also be purchased from arts and craft stores.

To each white card glue a piece of colored paper. Alternatively, using markers or pencil crayons, color one side of the index cards in the seven different colors. Leave one card plain. Leave the backs of the cards white except for perhaps a hand drawn picture or stencil of a dragonfly. An alternative to white backs, are to cover with a sticker, wrapping or metallic paper. Laminate the cards to protect the surface. You can also use wrapping tape to protect them by sandwiching the card between two strips of the wrapping tape and trimming the edges.

You should end up with eight cards of eight different colors. On the reverse side, it is white so that the face (the color) is obscured from the sitter. The color will be revealed once the card is turned.

Dragonfly Oracle Deck Meanings

Red Color Card — red is a warm color and is excellent for arthritic joints and stiffness in the body. Red promotes a sense of self-reliance and independence and it is also a color of passion and vitality. Red is associated with the root chakra, it is a power color. If you need courage to make changes or you need a boost of energy to get things done, bringing red into your life will help you. Red can also be used to ease depression and to burn out cancer, but is not to be used with people who have high blood pressure and should not be used for an extensive period of time.

Red: passion, leadership, active, better at making decisions. Red loves a challenge and desires success. Red as a spiritual color shows enthusiasm for faith and the desire to feel the presence of the divine within their bodies.

Orange Color Card — this color is warm and cheerful, it inspires us to take action and be unafraid to make the necessary changes we need to make. Orange is the color of abundance and resource-fulness but like red, it should not be used for a long time as it can cause restlessness.

Orange: radiates warmth and happiness, orange is the color of freedom and adventure. Orange is the "gut instinct" we should listen to.

Yellow Color Card — Yellow is helpful during intuitive work and helps to restore a person when their energy is drained. Bright yellow around the head is a very good sign. Yellow strengthens the mind and allows for clear, logical decisions. Yellow aids in digestion, liver and diabetes.

Yellow: clarity of thought, uplifting, illuminating, yellow is full of confidence and zest for knowledge.

Green Color Card — is a universal healing color; it has a powerful effect on the heart and the blood supply. Green helps mental processes, eases anxiety, heart and blood pressure problems. Green contains loving energy, so is useful when someone is dealing with relationship issues.

Green: is a color of balance and harmony, green can sympathize with the situations of others. Green is empathic and logical and gives us the ability to nurture ourselves and others.

Blue Color Card — is cooling and calming, it is good for anyone who suffers with diseases that are inflammatory and is healing for all issues around the throat and communication.

Blue: is the color of devotion, spirituality and serenity.

Indigo Color Card — helps with development of intuitive abilities such as clairvoyance. The color indigo helps with migraines, sleeping problems, lymphatic and immune system. Indigo should be used for shorter durations as it can cause feelings of being ungrounded in this reality.

Indigo: spiritual attainment, awareness, the unconscious and wisdom.

Violent Color Card — is beneficial brain and mental disorders such as depression. Violet stimulates feelings of inspiration, humility, and helps with dream recall. This is the color for spiritual work and spiritual wellbeing.

Violet: healing abilities, spiritual mastery, idealism and love for humanity

White Color Card— is balancing and restorative especially after any psychic work, it also creates a powerful protective shield from lower vibrations. White can be used universally like green for healing on all levels — mind, body, spirit and environment.

White: purity, innocence, cleanliness, new beginnings and clarity of purpose.

Meaning of the Seven Directions Cards

The **first** direction in the spread, deals with the central issue of the main focus, what are you dealing with right now or what's going on around you.

The **second** direction deals with related issues that are around the main focus.

The **third** direction is about the source of your problem, what's really going on and hidden influences and moon energy.

The **fourth** direction is comparable to a sunset; it is about what is receding in your life, what is leaving and the past.

The **fifth** direction is your assumptions, your beliefs, and it can also be what you desire to happen.

The **sixth** direction is how to best proceed, lesson to be learned, helpful advice.

The **seventh** direction is the future, possible outcomes, how you will end up feeling and developing issues.

How to do a reading can be found at the end of this chapter.

Earth Teachers Oracle Deck

Materials Needed:

30 index cards cut to the proper size that feels comfortable in your hand.

Markers or pencil crayons

Select your choices of decorating items such as pictures from magazines, wrapping paper or stencils. You don't have to place pictures on your cards; words will do just fine and work well without imagery.

The backs of the cards should all have the same design or be left plain, and on the front of the cards there could be an image, but whatever, there must be the names of plants and animals and the phrase that goes with it.

For example: on the face of the first card you would write "SAGE" either at the top or bottom and at either the top or bottom of the same card you would write the phrase "INNER KNOWING". You will need to follow this procedure with each of the 30 cards.

Once completed, use wrapping tape or laminate to protect the cards from damage, as with the Dragonfly Medicine Cards.

Card Meanings

Sage

Printed on the card: **Inner Knowing**
I am Sage, a voice in the desert, I am aware that my song is heard in the burning of my leaves. My power is of earth and sky. I was here before the humans walked this land. I have beheld the mysteries of the night and day. I felt the power when the summer and winter were created. My spirit has been called to help you with a message. My earth song is about wisdom and seeking knowledge from within.

Using inner wisdom brings forth a wealth of knowledge; this is a time to listen to your soul, so go within to find the answers. Dance and smudge, this will open you up spirituality and attune you to my energies. My wisdom is ancient, it is telling you to stop living in your dreams, get out of your head, you're thinking too much. You have an idea of the life you want, so go out and get it.

Divinatory Meaning of Sage
a) Life has settled into a somewhat boring routine right now and whether you realize it or not, your higher self is trying to tell

you that life is a sacred mysterious journey. So get in touch with the mystical aspects of creation.

b) A change of pace is coming, flow with it, embrace it.

c) You have or will be, shortly changing your attitude about a situation that has kept you back; people will show up in your life to give you a fresh perspective.

Sweetgrass

Printed on the card: **Friendship**

I am Sweetgrass, my smoke is mild and agreeable. Many plant people like me because of my amiable disposition and I attract many beings, such as the fairies who love my soft scent.

Where I grow, the ground becomes blessed and sweet. My spirit has been called upon to give you a message and I desire to share my earth song with you.

I can help with communications, and when I am called upon, I can sort out the detrimental people from the real friends.

Sweetgrass is telling you that there are people who are good for you so you need to make the effort to make new friends. This card also suggests that sometimes we lose connections with old friends and so this card reminds you to reconnect with these people.

Sweetgrass earth song is about making time to find peaceful places to meditate, slow down, spend quality time with less demanding people and get out and meet new friends.

Divinatory Meaning

a) Many people will be attracted to you; there will more invitations to gatherings and parties.

b) You will have the upper hand in gossip.

c) Certain relationships will become sweeter.

Cedar

Printed on the card: **Balance**

I am Cedar, I know my duty is protection and I provide safe harbor for wildlife. I also know that I keep humans alive even through the harshest of winter. I know my duty and I know my abilities. The Creator gave me to humanity to remind them of the gift of balance, of work and rest and of giving and receiving. My earth song is about balance and my spirit has been called today to give you this message.

Cedar is giving you the gift of fun and responsibility. This is a time for playtime and living up to responsibilities. You may be feeling a bit weary and fatigued, you need to look at your situation with fresh eyes and not see problems but opportunities. This is a time to create closer bonds with people in your life. And this is a time where you serve and learn the beauty of being of service to others, but it is also a time when you need to accept the help of others. In order to move through this phase in your life with ease is to appreciate the importance of receiving help and performing duties to others.

Divinatory Meaning

a) Focus on your responsibilities and spending time having fun.
b) Do some meditations and reading on how to achieve balance in your life.

Tobacco

Printed on the card: **Soul Journey**

I am tobacco. I hear your mortal cries for help. I will illuminate your path and even on the darkest of nights, my power is with you. I am a force to be reckoned with and no challenge is too big for me. I am strength, and the power of the Creator is within me. My earth song is passionate, the spirit of the eagle is within me, and I am within the eagle. I have been drawn to you today to give you this message.

You are in or entering a phase known as the dark night of the soul, sometimes spirit requires that we walk through darkness so that we may see our own inner light. The smallest candle can conquer blackness of the earth's tombs. Tobacco spirit has come to you to let you know that burning and meditating with this plant, can help you find the strength to carry on. From beneath the heaviness of depression, there emerges a light from Mother Earth, a plant whose earth song is a beacon of promise to all who are oppressed. Allow the darkness to come, there will always be a morning, a time when the anxiety eases. Offering tobacco at sunrise illuminates your spirit and lets you know troubled times are ending soon.

Divinatory Meaning

a) There is a conclusion ... an ending.
b) Time to break free and fly.
c) Being released to explore new options.

Lily Pad

Printed on card: **Worry**
I am Lily Pad and I am introverted and a worrier. I am usually preoccupied about what is going on around and under me, but I also know that I help others and I don't mind being of aid to someone as long as they don't abuse my help and drain me of my energy. My earth song is being comfortable with who you are. Our flaws make us unique and even if we are prone to self-doubt we still have much to offer. My spirit has been drawn to you today because you've been worried. There is a feeling that something is wrong and it nags at the back of your mind.

What lies beneath, what is hidden is troubling you. I do not recommend you meditating on the beautiful lily pad because it is often the victim of being anxious itself, but to instead meditate on all the creatures it gives shade to and how they appreciate it.

Divination Meaning

a) You are very worried about what is going on behind the scene.

b) Something is nagging you, a worrisome feeling.

c) Watch out for psychic vampires who could drain you mentally, emotionally and physically.

Fern

Printed on the card: **Distrust**

I am Fern and I onto hold secrets. I prefer to keep knowledge to myself. I can teach when you need to keep quiet and when to share with others. When I see humans with unspoken words buried deep within them, I release a wave of compassion, for I understand the burden of secrecy. My earth song is about secrets, an image or knowledge that is kept within the confines of my spirit. There are wishes and desires held within me, only a song from the purest of intentions can release me.

Drawing this card is suggesting that you are holding emotions within yourself and there is a symptom of distrust within you, perhaps you have hurt someone. Rely on the ability of the fern to bring a healing energy into situations where pain exists.

Divinatory Meaning

a) Regret.

b) Feeling like you have lost your best friend.

c) Loss.

Orris

Printed on the card: **Mystic and Mundane**

I am Orris and I am an all-knowing plant. The Creator gifted me with great psychic powers and I am confident in my visions and dreams. My earth song is that I have always thought humans were too preoccupied with the mundane. My song is about pausing in your daily routines to reflect, pray and pay close attention to what happens around you, you could be astonished to realize that woven within the mundane events of life there are silvery threads of the mystical.

You have been, or in the near future will be, evaluating your career. People are going to be coming into your life with news of job opportunities or ideas of where to find a job. Don't be surprised by the many coincidences that are happening; the Divine is sending you the right people, doors are opening and many things that were hidden are going to be revealed. Through this time of transitions, Mother Earth is helping you to be more spiritually aware of how people are connected and how synchronicity works.

Divinatory Meaning

a) Work and new opportunities.

b) Important communications concerning money.

c) Meeting the right connections to get you on the right track.

Belladonna

Printed on the card: **Solitude**

I am Belladonna, I am a being that is working on the healing of mental illness and sorrow. My song can be a mournful one. I walk on the edges of darkness, and the unknown doesn't frighten me. It is my path to travel between the worlds of sanity and madness. My spirit has been summoned today to give you this message.

You will now or in the future experience feeling cold inside, the wound you have been dealt has brought about a withdrawal from friends and family. Belladonna is a plant that really likes to be left alone and doesn't want to help people, gardens or animals, its path is one of solitude. Drawing this card means that your state is similar to being belladonna right now. The way out of the darkness is with a spirit of gratitude, you have come to the edge of your light and now the darkness stands in front of you like a wall of storm clouds.

Divinatory Meaning
a) Depression and possible illness.
b) Be aware of your fragile emotional state and seek help.
c) Stuck.

Tulip

Printed on the card: **Be a Friend**
I am Tulip, my earth song is reflective and I tend to be a melancholic flower. I accept that we beings of earth cannot be happy all the time and accepting that is peaceful. There are other beings who think I hide my sadness behind bright colors, which is not totally true, for if we don't experience sad days, how can we appreciate the happy ones.

Drawing this card is telling you that someone who is close to you is going through a difficult time and hiding it. If you are aware of who this is, try and help them through this difficult phase. If you believe this card is for you, the message is that the situation will become worse before it gets better, and if the second card is a positive card that improvement will happen within six months.

Divinatory Meaning
a) Helping self or others through a difficult time.

b) Getting worse before it gets better.

c) Finding a friend to talk with.

Mistletoe

Printed on card: **Intimacy**

I am Mistletoe, I am aware that I have been revered by humans for centuries. I have gained much wisdom from watching humans and I have come to know the human's soul. Intimacy is about being emotionally close to your partner. To be open, sharing and accepting of yourself and your lover.

Pulling this card means that you are becoming wiser about what is going on between you and someone you are close to.

You are entering a new phase where you must overcome obstacles using determination. A period and resolution and change is ahead. Meditate on mistletoe, this plant will aid you in your relationships with significant others. Mistletoe's energies will be with you to help you to find it easier to share some types of your feelings with others. Mistletoe is teaching that when you become sad and need some comforting, you will be able to allow yourself to be open to receive some nurturing from others.

Divinatory Meaning

a) Change of direction in relationships.

b) Unexpected responses.

c) Passion.

Dog

Printed on the card: **Health**

I am Dog totem, my earth song is about being fit and strong. I draw that energy from the Earth Mother so that I can pass it onto humans. I know that one must think ahead to survive and I have helped people to survive for hundreds of years. I am practical and I believe that one must be sensible to withstand all the trials that life can throw at us. My spiritual energies have been called upon to give you a message.

You have neglected your health for far too long, you are working too hard and doing too much for others. It is time to start to eat proper and exercise. Dog totem is very serious about wellbeing; this earth teacher knows it is important for humans to take care of themselves if they want to get the work done. Dog's temperament is all about self-care and self-awareness and to be active. This is the time to eat right and get moving.

Divinatory Meaning

a) Take care of your physical self.
b) Don't over indulge.
c) Don't go in too many directions.

Bee

Printed on the card: **Aware**
I am Bee and I am like a busy housewife; cooking, cleaning, aware of what goes on in my dominion. Nurturing others, and working very hard every day and loving every minute of it.

I am aware that we all need moments of quiet reflections so that we can see what is really going on. Awareness is knowing what is happening within you and around you. There can be activities that go on behind the scenes of our relationships and our jobs, if these activities affect us, it is important that we are aware of them so we can make appropriate changes. My earth song is trying to tell you that don't be so caught up in chores that you miss the sad expressions on a loved one's face or see the jealous glare from a workmate. Slow down and be aware there's a need for it. It could be someone or it could be a health issue.

Divinatory Meaning

a) Caution.

b) Be alert to hidden messages.

c) Don't take anyone for granted.

Bull (work)

Printed on the card: **Frugal**

I am Bull and I help your thoughts. I have wisdom for making things last as my disposition is hardy and I am made to endure. My earth song is all about endurance and being able to withstand the trials of life. I have been summoned today with a message of being careful with resources at hand. Be prepared to earn that extra money that will be needed.

I am an earth teacher who not only adds beauty to your life, but also imports a desire to be careful with money and other resources. I even encourage the wise use of water and the nutrients in the soil around me, for I know the importance of fertile earth. Having me as a totem will help you to be better at managing your life and making the best use of what you have. Meditating on me will ground you and will make you more money smart. Pulling this card suggests that the energy of abundance isn't really cut off, it is just not flowing as it should at this time, this is why mediating with Bull totem will help.

Divinatory Meaning

a) Problems and loses at work and home.

b) Time to be frugal and make the most of what you have.

Buffalo

Printed on the card: **Stability**

I am Buffalo, my medicine is peaceful and I am happiest living within a herd. The vibrations that come from me are positive and

I am here to enhance the feelings of stability and compassion to the human race. Meditating with my energy and enjoying my vibrations, stabilizes emotions and helps bring clarity to situations. My earth song is seeking inner peace through stability and being in a secure position.

My message to you is there are many benefits that come from being stable. Being stable isn't being boring; it is living from a place of unwavering belief and understanding of where you are at, mentally, emotionally and physically. You are about to enter into a state of being more stable, buffalo is the energy of stability and can help the transition from chaos to stable living.

Divinatory Meaning

a) Relationships are stable.

b) A time of smooth sailing, you are firmly established and not easily shaken.

c) All is quiet and good right now.

Snake

Printed on the card: **Blindness**

I am Snake and I am a being that prefers to be left alone. I am known in the animal world as being somewhat of a grouch. Having this card come up in a reading means that you are refusing to see a situation for what it is.

You are not being honest with yourself out of fear and shame. If you have pulled this card for a relationship, it means that you are in a self-destructive pattern with some people in your life. If you have pulled this around work, then it means that you need to assert self-control and resist the fear of change in order to move forward towards your goals.

Divinatory Meaning

a) You have or will be in a destructive relationship, seek help

and support from friends.
b) Don't ignore good advice from loved ones.
c) You will educate yourself and learn how to avoid unhealthy people and situations, but best to do this sooner than later.

Earth Worm

Printed on the card: **Plenty**
I am Earthworm and I love to be surrounded by beauty. I love being with other flowers and enjoy a garden of variety. Fairies love my work because I promote a healthy environment for beauty. I attract abundance, for my vibration is optimistic and so my energies align with receiving. Having me around and enjoying the benefits of my work will bring you many beautiful things, such as relaxation and serenity. No bountiful garden would be without me.

You are entering into a more secure time especially around finances, for you have worked hard either physically or mentally to achieve this state of stability. The rewards include being in a state of self-reliance and appreciation that your efforts have paid off, and that you can get what you hoped for. There is a sense of inner exuberance right now and this phase of richness will stay throughout the coming year.

There is also peace in your relationships, enjoy this period of happiness.

Divinatory Meaning
a) Fresh phase in life of abundance and happiness.
b) Being secure for the first time in a long time.

Spider

Printed on the card: **Secrets**
I am Spider and I am a rather peaceful being who loves to be in

tranquil surroundings. My earth song is earthy and sensuous. I love to be around loving vibrations. I can be somewhat secretive, so this card can foretell of someone close to you being tight-lipped about someone or something.

You are now or will be involved with some complicated people. You are so easy going and trusting that these new encounters will really make you step back and rethink relationships and messages received. Are you prepared for this?

Divinatory Meaning

a) Trust intuition about people.
b) Someone knows more than they are sharing.
c) Be a spider in the corner, observing.

Cardinal

Printed on the card: **Taking the Initiative**
Speak your mind.
Relationships.
I am Cardinal and I am strong medicine for the heart. The red in my wings displays how I enjoy healing all heart related issues in people. I am here to help heal your heart and bring stability to your feelings about the relationships in your life. It is time for you to speak your truth with love and compassion.

Divinatory Meaning

a) You have relationships in your life that need healing, some have to change in order to survive and others need to be dissolved for everyone's good.
b) You are having a change of heart about someone or something.

Moth

Printed on the card: **Be an Observer and Learn**
I am Moth totem. I teach that it is wise to be discreet and not lay all your cards on the table, and to be careful whom you talk to.

My earth song is about communications — dialogue between many types of beings that exist in many dimensions. This can mean that your guides and angels are trying to get your attention right now, so slow down listen to them. They desire to keep you on your chosen path, be open to dreams and images that appear to you.

You will be drawn to nighttime and gatherings by moonlight. There are others who have some interesting news about people that you know. Don't be gullible and believe everything you hear, but also be prepared to read between the lines of what people say.

Someone could reveal something to you that will help you reach much needed conclusions about someone or something

Divinatory Meaning
a) There are messages coming to you.
b) Secret meetings.
c) Running into people you know.
d) Odd alliances.

Bear

Printed on the card: **Boundaries**
I am Bear and I honor traditions. I believe that rituals are important to living beings. I feel happy to help to assist humans in finding happiness. My energy can sometimes be ferocious and that is a signal not to let people trample on your beliefs, and personal and family traditions.

Bear teaches that to know oneself and to respect oneself is very empowering. You are a sum total of your memories, your experiences and your traditions, so don't let others trample them.

This card also suggests you could be in a relationship or will be with someone who doesn't have the same values as you do. Don't give up your traditions, and don't change yourself to suit others.

Divinatory Meaning

a) Don't be such a people pleaser. Do what is best for you and loved ones.

b) Don't let someone dictate how to run your life. Someone could be trying to tell you that you should move, quit a job and so forth so make your own decisions.

c) If others are bullying you at work, school or home, read up on how to deal with controlling bullies.

Eagle

Printed on the card: **Good Process**

I am Eagle and I am ambitious. My earth song proclaims that I know the way to the top. I am Eagle and I can fly closest to the Creator and I wish to help you to attain your deepest desires. I like to be noticed. I am the natural achiever.

The spiritual world is bringing you to a place where only good things can emerge. This card reminds you to take one day at a time, but know that your soul is stretching and searching for knowledge even though you are unaware of it, answers are coming to you in dreams and in the people you meet. Your inner self is reaching for the sky, the promise of new growth and new opportunities are happening. There is increase in happiness and wealth in the coming months.

Divinatory Meaning

a) Opportunities are coming (as in more than one) so make sure you jump on them but remember to look and think before you leap.

b) Spirit is guiding you in how to move forward in the future.

c) Don't be afraid when someone gives you an idea, go home and mull it over.

Swan

Printed on the card: **Positive Partnerships**

I am Swan and I am quite aware that my strength and my life come from Mother Earth. I help others. I love to add beauty to things and I can attract love and friendships for you. I am aware that people have come to me for help and I can give it when I am dealt respect.

My energies come to you with a message … you will meet people with mutual goals and some will help you with the ideas that you have. This card foretells of a possible joint venture with someone you don't know, but will meet in the coming months, but it can also foretell of a possible romantic attachment.

Divinatory Meaning

a) You will be forming some strategic partnerships with some interesting results in the future.

b) Mother Earth will be bringing in positive energies into your relationships.

c) A friend will be bringing you some good news or a gift.

Wolf

Printed on the card: **Sacredness of Spirituality**

I am Wolf and my earth song is about the sacredness of your spirit. Sacredness manifests itself to each of us in its own unique way, the important thing is to honor it and uphold the sacred in your life. Chose a holistic lifestyle, this includes living in a manner where you feel like a whole person. Energy follows thought, so try to keep your thoughts on trust, love and acceptance. These practices can promote wellness in our bodies, minds and spirit.

Divinatory Meaning

a) Honor the spirit of nature.

b) Meditate on spirit.

c) Live holistically.

Horse

Printed on the card: **Gifts and Travel**
I am Horse and my earth song is about the wisdom of coming from a solid opinion based on facts and knowledge gained. For many years, I helped the people of Turtle Island get around. I helped the people explore, trade and find food.

My earth song is about travel, and gaining experiences through travel or communications. My song and message is also about being courageous and having enthusiasm to make your dreams come true.

Someone is going to loan you some money or a gift of money will come into your life. There will be travel in your future, but this will be a learning experience, learning things about yourself or others. There will be interesting moments around travel and some interesting news coming from afar.

Divinatory Meaning

a) A trip either physically or spirituality.

b) A time of rest and relaxation, enjoy yourself.

Butterfly

Printed on the card: **Transitions**
I am Butterfly and my earth song is about movement and experi-

ences. Our lives should not be stagnated, so be careful of who or what is influencing you. Your friends, family and workmates can pull you backward. Don't let others trample on your dreams. In the coming months you will be attracted to people and events that will add value to your life. Remember those dreams you had and the goals you wanted to accomplish, focus on them and make the effort to achieve them. Butterfly teaches that you will become more confident when you achieve your goals.

An important endeavor is coming up; you will sail through it smoothly. Butterfly totem's wish is for you to have a sense of thankfulness for the experience, and although this feeling of gratitude will be tinged with sadness, it will be a passage that is needed in your life.

Divinatory Meaning

a) Obstacles are being placed before you so that you must deal with issues you've not dealt with in the past

b) In the coming months you will be making some significant achievements in areas of self-improvement

Owl

Printed on the card: **Take a Closer Look**

I am Owl and I am a hunter and a natural detective. I will get to the bottom of things to find the solutions. There are issues going on that you just don't understand and it is driving you crazy. My earth song is about being unique and different. I do things in my own time and my cycles are designed to be my expression not following the pack. I am also into the details, and I am naturally curious, so when solutions seem to be unclear, my energies can help clear things up for you.

Things will be clearer in the near future but you will have to work to make this happen. Write down what is bothering you, talk to people you can trust. The energy of this card suggests that times will be tough for a while. This must happen because the universe is unraveling the problems and is trying to encourage you to find your own creativity in solving the challenges of your life lessons.

Divinatory Meaning

a) People will begin to notice your unique style.

b) Your suspicions are warranted, look closer at the situation.

Dolphin

Printed on the card: **Becoming Unstuck**

I am Dolphin and my earth song is all about becoming unstuck from a negative place. It is time to figure out how to move on. I live in the water yet I am a mammal and breathe air. I live in harmony between two worlds. I am here to tell you that you need to find that balance and harmony in your own life. Let go of clutter, let go of negative people, move forward to what you desire and even if the progress is slow that is fine just keep going.

Divinatory Meaning

a) Avoid blaming others it keeps you stuck.

b) Write down what you want.

c) Do something each day that is good for yourself.

Rowan Tree

Printed on the card: **Trust in Others**

I am the Rowan Tree. I am a strong plant being. I am not afraid of who I am and how I have evolved. I love to shelter other plants so I can watch over them. Very softly and clearly, I speak each plant being's name that shares my space and I assure them that they will never be alone again. The Creator has linked us all together in love and we must travel back to that memory of when we were first formed and give thanks.

Divinatory Meaning

a) There are those you can't trust, but do not forget that there are those that you can.

a) Sometimes you must reach out to others when you are in need.

Rose

Printed on the card: **Love**

I am Rose and I am beauty and pain. I am aware that life can be sweet and yet painful. I stand with my eyes closed and listen to the thoughts of the people. I long to take their pain away but I know I can't and so thorns appear on my stem. These represent the lessons and the sacrifices we all must make on our journeys.

I am Rose and my earth song is about love and matters of the heart. There is now, or will be, a bittersweet time. On the one hand, you will be getting what you wished for, on the other, you will be outgrowing a situation or person and there will be a desire to move on.

Divinatory Meaning

a) Beware there is a person/s that love is conditional; they withhold their love and affection, when you don't behave or act as they want.

b) You will be seeking the help of a friend or therapist in order to move.

Karma Cards

Materials Needed:

- 10 index cards cut to suit the size of your hand.

- Markers or pencil crayons.
- My cards have no images on them, I have only a written word printed onto them, but you could create an image for each card if you wish.
- Wrapping tape or laminate to protect the cards.

The Cards

Past life & Soul Purpose Card Meanings

1. ASSERTIVE

Past Life: in prior lifetimes you were dependent on others, and in this incarnation you are learning to be independent and make your own decisions, so there are lots of lessons and challenges around decision making. You did not feel capable enough to handle many responsibilities and looked to others for help. Situations where you needed to make choices frightened you.

Soul Purpose: is to forge ahead into unknown territory where people will look to you for answers and solutions.

The lesson of being assertive, speaking up for yourself and others, is being learned in this lifetime. Situations will present themselves that will teach you to have greater confidence in yourself.

2. BE YOURSELF

Past Life: in a prior lifetime, you were not allowed to speak your truth, you were told what to wear and where you could go. You suffered under much verbal and physical abuse and consequently, you grew to hate yourself and to have a very low opinion of yourself.

Soul Purpose: in this incarnation, you have a yearning to speak your truth. Your vibration is to nurture the seeds of originality within yourself and others. The Creator has called you into this world to bring creativity, co-operation, harmony, tolerance and promoting the rights of people and animals. Before you can do the work of the Creator, you must learn to love yourself, and by taking care of yourself, it will enable you to take care of others. Do not sacrifice your own dignity for others.

3. STEADFASTNESS

Past Life: scattered, unable to focus, "jack of all trades master of none", difficulty knowing what you wanted. You were very hard and very critical of yourself; you hindered your own growth. Although you loved being social and enjoyed the company of others, you often sought out the ideas of other people to help create a clearer mental picture of what you wanted. Even with scattered energies you were highly creative, loved good conversation and were quite inventive.

Soul Purpose: learning to focus your energies and to stick with a plan until it has been fulfilled. Sticking to a plan and seeing things and projects through until the end is a lesson that you are learning right now or will be facing in the future. You can change your mind quicker than a blink of an eye but this trait creates chaos in your life. Learning the art form of wise decision making is a lesson to be learned. Also a lesson to be learned in this incarnation is to slow down and take the time to recharge your batteries.

4. SECURITY

Past Life: a main focus in a prior lifetime was security for yourself and your family. In that prior lifetime, you were on a constant search for adequate money, food and shelter, the need to survive was powerful. It was a hard, a lifetime full of poverty and worry.

Soul Purpose: you have learned to be practical and frugal when necessary, although most of your decisions are made out of worry and fear of losing everything. You will be put into situations where you will take risks, although there will be an air of caution. You will learn issues around trust and attaining goals without anxiety.

5. FEAR OF ABANDONMENT

Past Life: you traveled, you had many adventures and you were often times the center of attention. You were very charming and could persuaded people into doing what you wanted. People often frowned on your lifestyle because it did not conform to society's standards, and as a result, many people came into your life and then left your life.

Soul Purpose: you love to be versatile, you love your freedom and time to relax and enjoy life's pleasures, but you need the closeness of others. Old soul memories of how people judged you on your unusual life, still subconsciously haunt you. You try to learn not to be ashamed of who you are and to cultivate a close circle of friends and family that you can count on, and who appreciate you for who you are. Learning lessons around fear of abandonment.

6. PEOPLE PLEASER

Past Life: pressure to be perfect and please everyone was an issue you lived with. People expected you to have all the answers and be able to solve all problems and be at a constant service to them. This put much stress on you, for people didn't consider your thoughts or feelings, they were inconsiderate and treated you like an abject instead of a person. Many lives were dependent on you for financial security and emotional security.

Soul Purpose: Learn how to deal with high expectations,

pressure from others and not being a people pleaser. In this incarnation, you will learn about healthy boundaries with people and not allowing others to control how you feel about yourself. You tend to do whatever it takes to please the people around you and you want everyone to be happy. You will be learning not to look outside yourself for validation, and knowing your values and priorities so that you can say a most important word ... no.

7. PATH OF AN EMPATH

Past Life: you were a mystic, a psychic, an occultist and studied alchemy. You enjoyed learning and seeking out new knowledge. You had healing abilities but you were a loner and tended to keep to yourself. You held a deep distrust of others motives, perhaps it was because you were empathic and could feel others feelings. The bonds you did make with others were deep though and fulfilling.

Soul Purpose: you must learn to trust others, you are a natural healer and you must learn to live life being an empath. Utilizing your intuitive gifts to help others and becoming more disciplined around your spiritual life will bring balance to your intuitive abilities. You must learn to channel the negative emotions from others away from yourself, those aren't your feelings, so let them go.

8. MONEY STORY

Past Life: You made money and you squandered money, but you had really good instincts of how to make money. In that prior incarnation, you experienced many ups and downs financially but usually landed back on your feet pretty fast.

Soul Purpose: You will be given lessons on handling money, respecting money, creating material wealth and being responsible with it. You will learn you are living under the karmic law of what you reap you shall sow. Life lessons coming up will be around realizing there are consequences for your actions.

9. HELPING OTHERS

Past lives: you did not respect the rights of others so much and you took much for granted in your life. It was a life that the focus was on self and you kept others at a fair distance as you were an extremely aloof person. You held sadness inside yourself and you did not live an authentic life. You had some very good qualities but you never nurtured them, you did what was expected of you.

Soul Purpose: you still distance yourself emotionally from others; close relationships are difficult for you. You hardly know who you are. It is time to take the time to know who you are and discover your values and beliefs. You will be given opportunities to help the rights of others including animals. Once you embark on being a positive force in your community, you will learn much about who you truly are.

10. WOUNDED HEALER

Past Life: many life times of hardship and devastation, you have learned lessons in giving as well as in taking. Those life times propelled you into a search for spiritual meaning and the reason for suffering. Adversity has made you who you are and you have learned many coping mechanisms to handle many types of challenges.

Soul Purpose: Eternity, wholeness, universal energies, mystic, encompassing all the traits of the numbers, old soul, potential, new level of learning, uncertainties, spiritual guidance, and ascending to the next level of non-being. You are at a new place for new lessons on a more evolved level. Your prominent talents are in care giving, counseling and helping others find their paths in life.

Enjoying the positive and negative aspects of past life effects. You learned it is better to give than to receive and this positive energy has broken down many negative actions from the past.

The Seven Directions Reading

The Seven Directions Reading is one of my original readings it is a three-part reading.

Part one is teaching the client about her healing color.

Part two is using cartomancy for an in-depth reading of what is going on in the person's life: I call this the heart of the reading because it deals with the mundane part of life that we all must cope with.

Part three is the client weaving their own life wheel of sacred directions, sacred colors and totems. At the end of the reading, the client will sit for a healing session and then select one last card from the Karma deck and the reading is done. The whole reading from start to finish takes approximately one hour.

PART ONE — Dragonfly Deck

The first part of the reading involves using the Dragonfly cards. I ask the client to be seated and I then shuffle the Dragonfly deck. I ask the sitter to select a card from it. If perhaps the client selected blue from the oracle deck, read from the book the meaning for the color blue. Tune into the color blue so that you go a bit further with developing your intuitive side.

In your mind's eye, visualize the client sitting in front of you and also the color blue. Imagine that the blue is magnetic and it will be drawn to the area where it feels a magnetic pull from the client's energy field.

If for instance the blue goes to my client's head, just off to her left side of her face, I let my mind relax and I ask "why is the blue attracted to this spot". I allow myself to feel the sensations coming from the blue at the side of her head. As I receive this information, I share it with my client. I might say to her "I sense blue is collecting around the side of your head, it is helping you with memory and advises you to not over exaggerate or under exaggerate past events".

Keeping my mind relaxed, I allow thoughts, words, and feelings to come to me concerning how the blue is affecting her body, her thoughts and her emotions.

I leave the color blue at her head, and with a painter's brush stroke, I visualize spreading the color blue around her surroundings. I imagine her looking at a home filled with blue things and I ask myself how my client might feel if blue was around her. I let my mind relax and I feel the color blue and how it would influence my client's health. If say I get a strong sense it would ground her feelings, help her mind be more focused and perhaps also help ease her anxieties, I share this with her.

I suggest you work with only one healing color during any one reading, as colors do change. Usually though a color remains with a person for between three to six months.

PART TWO — Cartomancy

I shuffle my playing cards and fan them out in front of my client I then ask her to select seven cards, which I arrange on the table right to left. I read the cards as I would read a story. At first, you will want to read the meanings of each card and that is okay but do try and use your psychic mind to interrupt the meanings of the cards. Remember you take all the knowledge from your inner mind and the cards are just a tool to pull that knowledge from you. It is important to understand the meaning of your cards, so you don't have to think about them anymore, but this takes time and practice.

1st card   The heart of the matter, message from the Creator.
2nd card   How you see yourself.
3rd card   Your earth walk, what you should be or not be doing.
4th card   Your strengths.
5th card   Your weakness.
6th card   Your higher purpose.
7th card   Future.

PART THREE — Dragonfly Medicine

After I am finished the Seven Directions Reading, I put the playing cards away and bring out the Dragonfly cards. I explain to my client that our thoughts and our behavior manifest as colors in our aura. I explain to them that when they are using the oracle deck, we select a card without looking at it, just as we did in the Seven Directions reading. Therefore we are allowing our higher self to pick the card that shows what color is resonating in different areas of our lives. Knowing this information brings insight to who we are. When the colors of your energy are laid out before you, it gives an interesting perception of yourself and increases your self-awareness.

I take four Dragonfly color cards and place them face down. I fan them out before the client, and ask the client to close their eyes and imagine they are facing **East**. I say a prayer to the Creator to show them what color their spirituality is resonating with.
    I then ask them to select a card.

I invite the client to imagine they are facing **South** and I ask the Creator to show them what color is resonating with their emotional health. I then invite the client to select a card for the southern direction.

Next I ask them to imagine facing **West** and I ask the Creator to show them what color is resonating with their physical health. I invite them to select a card.

Lastly, I ask them to face **North** and I ask the Creator to reveal to them what color represents their mental state and the sitter selects a card.

I then lay all the cards out in a circle for the client to see. I explain to them that each direction represents a facet of themselves. East is their spiritual nature, South is their emotional nature, West is their physical nature and North is their mental nature. Using the card meanings, I share with them what each color represents.

For example, the client selected a card in the color red for East. The card's meaning is about passion and independence this tells her that at this moment her feelings around spirituality revolve around her passion for freedom, she is keen to discover her spiritual path independent of any organized religion. Red experiences the divine when engaged in a physical activity such as hiking in nature.

After I have finished with the color cards, I bring forth my Earth Teacher Cards and spread them out in front of the client. I follow the same process as with the Dragonfly cards. Accordingly, there should be one totem card in each of the four directions.

For example, I ask my client to close her eyes again and imagine she is looking East. I say a prayer for her and ask her to select a card. If say my client selects Cedar from the Earth Teachers deck, keeping in the eastern direction, I now look the card. Cedar is about balance, it is important that we make time for our physical, mental, emotional and spiritual life. If one area becomes neglected or if we obsess about one area, our wheel becomes unbalanced. Sacred Earth Teacher therefore is Cedar for the Eastern direction of her Life Wheel. This process is done in each of the four cardinal directions.

At the end of the reading, I perform a healing ritual with the client. After the ritual is over the client can select a card from the Karma deck, this brings the Seven Directions Reading to a close.

Chapter 11

Healing Ritual

I perform this ritual on my clients after a reading for healing and balance.

After a reading, using my cards, I ask the person to sit comfortably in a chair and relax. Next, I ask the angels and ancestors to come and assist in the healing.

You can do the same. Then carefully place your herbs in a shell or fireproof container. As you light them, say a silent prayer for this person to be healed. Fan the smoke around the person's body starting at the feet and working your way up and around till you come to the head, and then ask the person to cup the smoke give a prayer of thanks for the healing and bring the smoke to their heart.

Performing this ritual cleans the person's energy field that surrounds them, brings healing to their hearts and it grounds their energies.

Preparing myself and my client for ritual

To prepare, I smudge myself and ask for protection, next I will imagine a sphere of light in my head and I watch it glow with love and purity and then I bring it down through my throat, chest and legs. I watch as the whole ball of light encompasses my whole being. I then bring my hands to my chest and give thanks.

Working with a client

Select a card for your healing from the color deck and use the color that is drawn in the healing ritual. In this example, I have used the color blue.

First, I will ask the person who is receiving healing to assist me in bringing in the color blue. We will both imagine a beautiful shower of blue falling all around them. The color permeates the whole person. I hold the intention that negative energy is being destroyed and driven away from the person and the room.

You can use any color you wish for this healing technique:

Place four blue candles around the person needing the healing. I place a candle in sand for earth, float candles in water for the water element, another candle represents the fire element, and feathers surrounding a blue candle for air and incense burning are for spirit. It is important to have all elements represented in your circle of healing because this brings about balance.

Once my client is sitting inside a circle of blue candles and all the elements represented the healing ritual can begin.

I light the first candle for **earth** and I acknowledge earth is fertile, stable and nurturing. I ask the angels of the earth to bring stability, from the richness of our Earth Mother and I ask for health and healing for my client.

Ask the client to make this vow (if they feel comfortable in doing so):

I vow to the earthly angels and to Mother Earth to be aware of the seasons and bounty of this earth and to be grateful for what I have. I vow to be mindful of the precious gift of life that my Earth Mother gives me and to show respect for all living things including respect for myself.

I light the blue candle with feathers around it for **air**. I acknowledge that air is light, life sustaining and energizing. I ask the angels of air to bring health and healing to my client's lungs and all the cells within my client's body. I ask the angels of air to bring in their gentle breezes to carry my client's prayers to the Creator with a message of thanksgiving for their life and their healing.

I light a blue candle for **fire**. I acknowledge that fire is renewing, purifying and creative. I ask the angels of fire to bring warmth and creativity into my client's life so that they can learn and grow to be happy and ask that the holy fire of God, burn all sickness within them and around them.

I light my floating candles and acknowledge that **water** is intuitive, soothing and cleansing. I ask the angels of water for the healing of my client's blood, kidneys and organs, and I pray for all the waters of Mother Earth to be cleansed and healed. I ask the angels of water to gift my client with intuition and allow my client's life to flow smoothly.

I light a candle or incense for **ether**. I acknowledge that ether is peace of mind, the divine presence and divine love. I ask the angels of the Holy Spirit to heal my client, guide them, renew them, and to uphold my client's life and my safety by the power of the Creator.

Chapter 12

Doing a Reading

Cartomancy, also known as metasymbology, is a form of divination using a deck of cards. This practice has been ongoing for hundreds of years for predicting the future and is now used as a tool for healing.

For the first style of reading, I use the standard 52 card deck, the four suits mirror the four seasons and the four elements, the twelve crown cards mirror the twelve months of the year, 52 cards for the 52 weeks of the year.

Your cards should not be used to play games keep these cards separate and treat them with care and respect. Smudge them after a reading and keep a quartz crystal on them to keep the energy around them pure and filled with light. Program your crystal to do this, bring your crystal to your heart and place the intention into the stone to protect the psychic energy around the cards.

If you are doing a reading in your own home, make sure the area that you will be working in is clean and tidy. Unnecessary items only stagnant the energy and get in way when you are trying to lay out cards, write things down or have a recorder handy.

Be sure the area is private and you have selected a quiet time for your client to come to your home.

Before I begin, I smudge the area, cards, and myself and then lay my protection crystals around me, such as rose quartz and amethyst. I follow this up by performing a meditation for protection and guidance.

When my client arrives, I usher them into the space where I'd like them to sit, and then make myself comfortable. Perhaps you might like to do the same.

To begin your reading, shuffle your deck and while you are doing this just let your mind relax and focus your client's energy. FEEL them with your heart. Take a couple of deep breaths, sending some oxygen to your brain, and then (this is the tricky part) I want you to connect with your client mentally, emotionally and spirituality, to feel how that person is feeling at that moment. There will be a prominent personality trait or mental or emotional state that you will feel.

Here is a sample reading:

After I have smudged myself and my client we sit down for the reading. I say a prayer to the angels, light my candle, perform the short meditation for the elements, fan out my Dragonfly oracle deck and ask the client to select a card.

After the client as selected a card they pass it to me and I turn it over. Let's say that the client has selected the green color card. I will share with them the meaning of this color and then I will *feel* the color green and them together. I will look away and I will visualize the person standing in front of me. I then make them small so I can take in their entire physical frame easily. It's like looking at a picture. I tell myself I want to see what is around them and I want to see where this color green flows to.

Once I am looking at them in my mind's eye, I will bring a tiny bit of green into my lower right vision and I will let it travel to where it wants to on the client. I watch where it wants to go. Perhaps I see it go to the knee and feet area and hear the word "grounding". If so I let the energy of that feeling hold my attention for a while until I get something more. Perhaps I then feel the energy of the color with the client and also protection. I let sensations come to me, also images and words and I may ask the client how they feel and if they need to be spirituality protected.

This is how I do it, it might seem slow to you at first but it will become much faster as you practice. It is linking energies and it is linking feelings and knowing when to pull back. I spend about five or ten minutes with this and I'll let my client know what I feel about the color and I will advice them to use it around them. If green isn't a color my client would normally use, I suggest bringing it in as accessories in their home such as in pillows.

Quick Meditation with Color

Imagine a shower of green water falling softy all around you. The shower is gentle and warm. The feeling is soothing and warm to the skin, the green glistens and sparkles. The radiant green engulfs you. You glow in this beautiful color green.

Performing a Readings for Others

I have walked a spiritual path for many years, in my book, *Walking the Path: The Cree to the Celtic,* I share my rituals and ceremonies that I use for healing myself and others. When I create a sacred space for ritual, I prepare myself and the area with prayers and smudging. The goal of a ceremony is to make medicine, in other words the goal is to encourage healing, to till the soil so seedlings of wellness spring up.

Years ago, I meditated and prayed about what direction I would like to go in with my spiritual path. I knew that a large part of my life would be performing ritual and sending out healing prayers for this world. Moreover, there were people on my path that influenced me to become a reader, including the Elder who blessed me, my mother who believed in my abilities, and the 200-year-old lady by the swamp.

Divination is a tool I use to bring healing for others and myself. It has been a complimentary companion to my ceremonies, and after every ritual, I carry out divination for healing and guidance. You don't have to perform a ceremony, but when you smudge and pray, not only do you raise your vibration, but you raise the vibration of the room, you create sacred energies and you draw in beings of light who only want to love and help you.

I started out doing readings for close friends and myself but then I knew that the Creator was bringing people to me for readings. After meditating on it, I did decide to charge for my readings, because as I have stated before, it is hard work and so the fair exchange for a job done. Being paid for readings is balance.

I began to hold parties once I felt ready, knew my cards, felt comfortable with them and had practiced my intuitive skills. I just knew I was ready. It will be the same with you, once you know your cards, practice your psychic skills, and have performed readings for friends.

Here is a nice little suggestion for you. Friends online can be a great place to practice. Just tell your buddies that you'll pull a few cards for them, they'll be lined up all day long and I can promise you that you'll get many opportunities for practice.

Many of us readers do house parties and good rule of thumb is to keep those first parties small. This is so you don't feel overwhelmed and you don't become too tired. In some gatherings, I will ask if a client would like to have a healing ritual, and in other gatherings I might not offer this, such as if it is for a corporate event.

Don't let clients talk you into a number of people that is beyond what you feel is comfortable. When I started out I didn't know any better and so I booked a party for eleven and I thought I'd pass out. I was so tired half way through that I honestly don't know how I finished those last readings. Even now, eleven readings in one day is a lot of people to tune into. Also always make sure you get the proper address and call back a day before the party to see if everything is still a go, you wouldn't want to drive there to find out they have changed their minds.

Depending on where you live, keep an eye out for weather reports. If you think there will be bad weather, let them know and always arrange a rain date in case of bad weather. Being a woman, I would never book a party if a man called. I have had men call and I have told them I do female only parties and insist that a female get back to me (in case they want a mixture of men and women at the party). Just let them know this is a safety issue and if they have a problem with it then it's probably not somewhere you'd want to go anyway. Always let friends and family know where you are going and when you'll be back. Carry a cell phone with you and if something doesn't feel right, don't do it, or don't go.

There are always those tricky questions that will be asked by clients, and how to deal with them is the difference between sailing through a reading or being stuck in a difficult situation and perhaps worrying about how you answered it later on. The first thing to remember if you are holding a party is do you really want to upset people who have gathered together to share food and drink? Remember you're doing a "party" where people are gathering to have fun; this isn't the time to give bad news. Remember, sooner or later you will have to emerge from your room to face a room full of people and no one wants to see a roomful of gloomy people. Now you might be asking yourself does this author say I should lie. Definitely do not lie to people but there are ways you can put things and you can choose not to share certain information and that is not lying. For instance, if you are tuning into someone and you feel that her friends that are in the next room are backstabbing her, I would suggest that you leave that out of the reading.

Then there is the question of letting someone know if their spouse is cheating on them. My friend who is a reader and who first taught me the cards will divulge that information in a reading. I feel it is not ethical to do so. What I tell people is that I am not doing readings to break up marriages or to hurt people's feelings, if they think a partner is cheating on them then they need to listen to their own inner voice and go with it. Also you don't want to give a reading that is biased, you can't tell people to quit smoking or give any of your own advice or personal opinions, they want your "psychic abilities" you should remember to work in the intuitive realms only.

When you are developing your intuitive abilities, you may become tempted to glance into people's personal lives. You will soon realize that you can see all of people's traumas, fears and other things. Beware of this kind of intrusion into the lives of others for it can leave you feeling overwhelmed by others remorse's and despair.

I'd like to add here that when holding a house party it is not the place to perform a healing session with the cards. People have gathered for fun and chitchat and so keep things light. If you see something in the cards or feel something with a person, you can ask them to come and have a private reading another time with you. I usually do my healing sessions when someone comes to my home and I know we'll have time and privacy, but there are parties that have likeminded people who are interested in healings.

Always walk in love, always have the intention to spread compassion and hope, divination can be used as medicine to bring enlightenment. The old saying of "the cards are never wrong" in my opinion is true but can we interpret the cards without being biased is the challenge. Be open to the energy you create in your sacred place and be aware of how the energies flow. Listen to your heart for it is NEVER wrong and walk in truth. Remember psychic development does take work, but of course anything worth having does require work.

Additional Tips

If you're reading several people, take your watch off and lay it beside your paper or tape recorder and mark the time that the client sat down with you so that you know how long you've been with them. Don't go over your allotted time with a client, it's unfair to you and it's unfair to the people who are waiting for a reading. You do not want people to become dependent on you, so if they want to book a reading with you again quickly, just explain to them that things need to settle and you can't see them again for six months. This way you will keep yourself free from psychic addicts. Many people are in a vulnerable state of mind when they go to see a psychic, there is often something traumatic going on in their lives and so you need to be emotionally grounded and keep the reading neutral. Always suggest to clients that are experiencing challenging times in their lives, to seek professional help.

Don't stay after the readings and socialize, because what tends to happen is that the people there will just keep asking you questions and you'll be totally drained of energy which is unhealthy for you.

Really consider long and hard before adding clients to things such as facebook, what sometimes happens is that you'll just get constant messages asking you to tune into this situation or this person and it gets really old fast. These are measures that I have taken in order to continue to enjoy doing readings, and it is good for people to respect the boundaries of you and of other people.

Just to sum up, before a client sits down with me there are a few things that I do. If I am reading in my home I smudge myself and my home, and I use my spiritual protection around myself, my home and my family including pets. I say a prayer for guidance and a blessing for the person I am reading and do a blessing for myself that I will be able to serve this person for their higher good. I turn off my phone and I try to arrange my readings when I know my family isn't around I select quiet times. Remember, in order to be able to tune in your mind, you must be quiet and relaxed so it's super important to not read on days when you are very hectic.

I like to have all my cards and crystals ready and also my recorder or paper and pencil, just in case I want to write something down. When the clients arrive, I offer them a glass of water or tea to help them relax and feel comfortable.

After reading each client, place a crystal on top of each deck of cards used. This practice keeps the energies clear and cleans up any attachments around the decks of cards.

You can develop your own psychic predictions business from your home. You can perhaps join a team of telephone readers. You can travel if you like and do home parties. As a reader, you may wish to remain within a sensible two hour traveling distance from your home or you can join a psychic fair group and travel across country.

Most of your clients will be women of various ages, so it is a good idea to keep track of their names, address, emails and phone numbers, so that perhaps every six months you can contact them to let them know if you are having any specials. Additionally, if you have added any new services to your business, you can let them know and send them positive affirmations to help them on their journey and to maintain that business connection with them. Do not be surprised at the huge chuck of expense you'll pay out in advertising, so it is wise to come up with new and innovative resources in your local area that provide cheap or free advertising. There may not be enough people in your local area to sustain you financially with steady readings, so do look into the option of performing readings on the phone and online. Consider making an appointment with a tax accountant to learn what is deductible and what is not and educate yourself on business taxes.

Having your own website is crucial to getting your business known and your name out there to potential clients. Many New Age stores like to have psychic readers come into their business establishments and perform readings, and so it would be a wise business move to send flyers to local business that could be interested in your services.

You may want to learn new techniques such as skrying, tarot, palmistry or divination with crystals and runes. It is a good idea to always be exploring new ideas and attending workshops to hone your skills and to develop new ones. Do not forget to add any new certificates or programs that you have attended to your credentials as a reader.

The best part of doing this work is making a difference in someone's life, remember divination can be a tool to empower us and give us direction. Developing as a psychic is all about listening to your inner knowing and trusting your intuition.

Dodona Books offers a broad spectrum of divination systems to suit all, including Astrology, Tarot, Runes, Ogham, Palmistry, Dream Interpretation, Scrying, Dowsing, I Ching, Numerology, Angels and Faeries, Tasseomancy and Introspection.